M

Paris
TIMES EIGHT

FINDING MYSELF
in THE CITY *of* DREAMS

Deirdre Kelly

GREY*S*TONE BOOKS

D&M PUBLISHERS INC.
VANCOUVER/TORONTO/BERKELEY

Greystone Books
An imprint of D&M Publishers Inc.
2323 Quebec Street, Suite 201
Vancouver BC Canada V5T 4S7
www.greystonebooks.com

Library and Archives Canada Cataloguing in Publication
Kelly, Deirdre, 1960–
Paris times eight : finding myself in the City of Dreams / Deirdre Kelly.

ISBN 978-1-55365-268-7

1. Kelly, Deirdre, 1960–. 2. Paris (France)—Social life and customs.
3. Paris (France)—Biography. 4. Journalists—Canada—Biography.
I. Title.
DC705.K44A3 2009   070.92   C2009-903861-7

Editing by Susan Folkins
Copyediting by Eve Rickert
Cover and text design by Ingrid Paulson
Cover illustration © Terra Standard/Free Agents Limited/CORBIS
Printed and bound in Canada by Friesens
Printed on paper that comes from sustainable
forests managed under the Forest Stewardship Council
Distributed in the U.S. by Publishers Group West

We gratefully acknowledge the financial support of the Canada Council
for the Arts, the British Columbia Arts Council, the Province of
British Columbia through the Book Publishing Tax Credit, and the
Government of Canada through the Book Publishing Industry Development
Program (BPIDP) for our publishing activities.

Mixed Sources
Cert no. SW-COC-001271
© 1996 FSC
FSC

To my mother, who said,
Because I know you can . . .

CONTENTS

Acknowledgments ix
Prologue 1

ONE · Au Pair, 1979 11
TWO · Wannabe, 1983 53
THREE · Material Girl, 1986 91
FOUR · Daughter, 1986 125
FIVE · Miss Lonelyhearts, 1990 163
SIX · Fiancée, 1995 209
SEVEN · Fashionista, 2000 241
EIGHT · Mother, 2007 275

ACKNOWLEDGMENTS

I WOULD LIKE to thank Susan Walker, recently dance writer for *The Toronto Star,* and Carol Toller, a trusted editor and steadfast colleague at *The Globe and Mail.* Both read early versions of the manuscript, and their constructive criticism and enthusiasm helped guide me forward at the beginning.

Cameron Tolton, my former professor at the University of Toronto, served, as he has selflessly done for the last thirty years, as mentor and confidant, even going as far as to confirm that I was right in wanting to celebrate the enduring allure of Paris when he offered at the Royal Ontario Museum a miniseries of public lectures on Paris films.

A heartfelt thank-you also to Salah Bachir, president of Cineplex Media, whose longtime friendship and generosity of spirit helped see me through much of the writing process, Jeffrey Sack, the lawyer who took my case at *The Globe and Mail;* Dr. Vera Victoria Madison for her invaluable advice; and Arline Malakian, Franco Mirabelli and Jackie Gideon for their eager support of the project.

My gratitude also to my agent, Hilary McMahon of Westwood Creative Artists, who tirelessly encouraged me. And to Bruce Westwood, a committed Francophile who said writing well is the best revenge.

Thanks also to Jennifer Barclay and Amy Logan Holmes, who published my first exploration of Paris as a literary subject in their jointly edited book, AWOL.

Rob Sanders and Nancy Flight of Greystone Books were the biggest supporters of this book. They never stopped believing in me, even when I didn't, and gave me all the time and hand-holding I needed to get it completed.

They were also responsible for introducing me to Susan Folkins, a gifted editor whose expert eye and highly attuned ear helped give the book a heightened clarity and shape. I thank her for all her hard work and passion. The next *kir*'s on me!

Thanks also to my younger brother, Kevin Kelly, who played audience to my first stories when we were small. And to my mother-in-law, Desanka Barac, for always wanting to lend a hand.

Finally, thank-you to my husband, Victor Barac, who listened and empathized and suggested and nodded in all the right places. He is my beacon, the one who showed me that one true journey is the journey of love. To him I give thanks also for our two beautiful children, Vladimir and Isadora Barac. The perfection of them, their precious sweetness, inspired me to want to create something everlasting. Something to make them proud.

PROLOGUE

"LIFE IS A process of becoming, a combination of states we have to go through. Where people fail is that they wish to elect a state and remain in it. This is a kind of death." I cupped my palm around these words in hopes that my mother, sitting next to me in the car, hands hawkishly grasping the wheel, would not see what was making me open my eyes in wonder. I didn't have to worry. Her mind was on her driving, or rather speeding—we had less than five hours to make it to Montreal, and we were racing against the eastbound Highway 401 traffic.

My mother isn't what you would call a bookish person. She doesn't entirely respect books and has never understood my passion for them. "You've always got your nose stuck in some book," she would say. Or, "Stop reading so much and go outside. You're pasty-faced." Or, "You think everything's in a book? Get real."

But books were my salvation, an escape from my family, which included a runaway father, a volatile mother, a wayward brother, an emotionally vacant maternal grandmother, and a grandfather who, my mother alleges, molested his own children, including her, while drunk. Not exactly a fairy tale, unless we're talking the Brothers Grimm. I found kindred spirits in books. They were the one place where my mother couldn't intrude and where I could escape my loneliness and sadness, forget my hurts, conceal my fears, and rise above my shame.

Now—ironically, with my mother as chauffeur—I was physically in flight. It was the summer of 1979. I had just graduated from high school, and to mark the end of what seemed an interminable childhood, I was departing Canada for Paris for my first visit there, at the invitation of Jenna and Nigel,* a Canadian couple who had asked me to help look after their two young boys. I was anticipating a reprieve from all that tormented me—my mother's complicated love and my own deeply sorrowful self. But the book in my hand, Anaïs Nin's study of D.H. Lawrence, was making the break difficult.

....

* Most names have been changed.

Nin's unhappy family life made me think of my own. My mother was always in the driver's seat. But though she might be driving, I was fiercely driven, determined to define myself in opposition to a person who was always telling me I was just like her—a chip off the old block. This notion mortified me.

When I was growing up, my mother wore hot pants and orange fishnet stockings, walked with a wiggle in her step should we go to a restaurant with one of her paying boyfriends, and ordered frosty mint-green grasshopper cocktails with paper umbrellas. She was a hot tamale. Men wanted her, I knew. She often told me that the husbands of her girlfriends would hit on her and that she would have to put them in their place. I didn't want to know this, but she said she had no one else to tell. And so I understood her to be a sex kitten but not a floozy. Still, seeing my mother in any kind of sexual light nauseated me. I couldn't articulate it at the time, but I wanted a mother who was nurturing, not naughty. A mother who was present, there for me, instead of the other way around.

She wore her streaked brown hair short now, with a chunk of bangs falling over one eye like Natalie Wood's (her favorite actress since she was young and saw *Marjorie Morningstar*). She cut it herself, often with a razor blade, slashing away at the back of her neck to correct what some idiot hairdresser had done. No one ever got it right with her. She had hazel eyes that she frequently narrowed to a piercing glare, and a prominent Presbyterian nose that, as she might say, was frequently out of joint. She wore too many gold rings at a time, one, sometimes two, to a finger, even though her hands weren't her best feature. She picked at them, tearing at the skin around the nails until it was raw. I never knew her to wear nail polish or eye shadow or perfume. Lipstick she liked, shades called Chiffon and Pearl Praline. The colors complemented her fair, flawless complexion, making her beautiful in her own way, I thought as I watched her hunched at the wheel, driving with her chest practically thrust upon the steering wheel—like a battering ram wheeling down the highway.

Partly she drove that way because of her height. She was five-foot-three to my five-foot-six and couldn't see out the window without propping herself up. But it was also a style of physical combativeness that she had perfected over the years. She was a jock, a field hockey player to be precise, whose bellicose ways with a stick had enabled her to hold her own.

Her bald independence and aggressive behavior had given her alpha-female ways some harsh masculine coloring. Even on the highway she was not exactly acting like a lady. "Get the hell outta my way!" she screamed at a driver in front of her. "Goddamn man! Did you see that?"

She leaned heavily on the horn and waved her arms angrily. I retreated into my book, trying to shut her out.

I had friends with more traditional moms who thought mine cool for seeming to be so liberated. But they didn't know what they were talking about. I hated having a single mom, hated being left alone at home while she was sleeping around, going out dancing, staying out without calling home. I waited and read and worried.

When she had spent all her money, she came to me for a loan. She said she was exhausted, on the verge of a nervous breakdown, and needed all I had to buy a ticket to Bermuda. Doctor's orders. I was devastated.

I had been scrupulously saving for months to get to Paris and away from her, doing any number of low-paying jobs after school and on weekends just to make sure I had enough. I had read Gertrude Stein's *The Autobiography of Alice B. Toklas* and imagined Paris as a place where art was king and the only rule was being true to yourself. I imagined aimless strolls down wide avenues and dapper Frenchmen bowing to kiss my hand. I imagined Paris to be a city where I would, for once in my life, feel free. It was no accident that for my dream city I chose a place that was physically and culturally as far away from my mother as possible. But when she asked for the money, how could I refuse? Of course I needed to help her. It was my responsibility. I was the kind of daughter who did as she was told. I put Paris on hold. I told the Canadians that I wouldn't be able to make it. They'd have to find a new babysitter.

But then my mother surprised me.

Instead of paying me back, she bought me the ticket to Paris. That was why we were now driving to Montreal. It had been a cheap fare, about $100 less than flying from Toronto—cheap on paper anyway. She hadn't factored in the cost of gas or the time spent driving such a vast distance to save a few dollars. But that was her—always looking for a bargain, but impulsively, erratically. She chortled that we were having an adventure. I read on, or pretended to.

But the book in hand was leading me down the thorny path of sex, sex, sex—sex in Paris, to be precise. Sex was usually something I tried strenuously to avoid. I wasn't entirely a sexual person; I was too consumed by fear to give myself up to the call of the wild. Sex was something that could lead to pregnancy, and pregnancy meant disaster, the end of your ambition and of your life. My mother had taught me that. She had become pregnant with me when she was nineteen, the same age as I was now.

She had never been interested in my father except for the fact that he had nice dark hair and strong eyebrows, qualities that she had hoped would pass on her to child. "And you do have nice eyebrows, you know. So I wasn't wrong about that."

He was what today is known as a donor, except he hadn't a clue. He had married my mother for love, she told me. He loved you too, she said. But he was gone by the time I was six.

"Aw, he just loved you too much. That's why he left. It hurt him. He loved his kids."

Her words left me completely bewildered. He loved me but had to leave me.

Love and desertion, love and hurt. I would always make the connection.

Now, as we raced to get me off to Paris, a city she had never been to yet imagined to be wonderful, full of promise, my mother screamed at me, "You are living my dreams! Don't ever forget that!"

Her voice clanged in my brain like a gong. I was paying attention to her now. She had pressed her body even tighter into the steering wheel. Her hands were fists, white at the knuckles. Suddenly she leaned on the horn. She began raging at a passing driver. But this time she apologized for her outburst. This shocked me; she never said sorry to anyone.

She rooted in her handbag on the floor next to her and pulled out a small packet of pills. "I'm sorry. I'm sorry," she said. Her voice sounded frantic. "It's a Valium. I have to take it."

She had never revealed a dependency to me before. She prided herself on never having touched a drink before she was twenty-eight, of never having smoked and having stayed away from drugs. But here she was now, sedating herself. She was strong! She was in control! And so her pronouncement unnerved me—the more so because she was still driving.

We had crossed the border into Quebec some time ago. The signs said *aéroport* instead of airport. The distance was now just twenty miles. I suddenly became aware that this was it, the end of our journey together. I wondered if I would miss her. But I didn't want to think about that now. I closed the book that had been sitting on my lap for hours, mostly unread. My mother was also strangely quiet. Maybe it was the pills she had just popped, or maybe it was the realization that I was finally going.

Approaching Dorval airport, we suspended our ongoing family drama to focus on the more mundane matter of getting me to my flight on time. Where was the exit for international flights? Where was the gate? My mother didn't want to pay the steep airport parking fees and so screeched to stop outside the terminal's sliding doors. We yanked my baggage out of the trunk and ran. We found the counter easily enough and were panting as I handed over my tickets. The agent told me where the departure lounge was and to be quick. Mother and I ran to the security wall and then, suddenly, it was time to part.

We looked at each other awkwardly. Who would reach out first? Neither of us was good at this anymore, not like when I was a little girl, eagerly flinging my arms around her neck and crying, "Oh, mommy!"

I think she, like me, was biting back tears. I had that panicked feeling again. What if I never saw her again? She was my tormentor, but she was the only family I had. "See Paris," she said, her voice strained. "Have fun. Have fun for me."

On that point, I thought, I won't let her down. Away from her and her suffocating ways, Paris was where I would find freedom. Even happiness. I already envisioned it as my dream city. The light at the end of my road. I willed myself not to cry, and stepped forward, past two uniformed men with electronic wands scanning my body for hidden weapons. They couldn't detect my breaking heart. I feebly waved to my mother and walked on, with Paris, my destination, before me, and my life in Toronto at my back. When I looked around again, my mother was gone.

ONE

Au pair

· 1979 ·

ON THE PLANE I shoved my face against the window and hoped that no one would see the tears streaking my face. I took out my journal, my constant companion since I was ten years old, and started scribbling. I tried reading Anaïs Nin again, her tales of desire and debauchery in Paris. Oh, I would never measure up.

A couple had settled in next to me. Their coziness, their two against my one, made me withdraw even more deeply into myself. Eventually I slept, but fitfully, and stirred only hours later when the captain announced our descent into Paris.

Deplaning at Charles de Gaulle airport, I desperately sought proof of the city's uniqueness, its enviable otherness, in the faces of every one of the baggage handlers, customs agents, and custodians buzzing around me. Was this the national character? I scrutinized the unsmiling faces, the black and bushy eyebrows knit in consternation. And then, waiting for my baggage, I saw the women, real *parisiennes*, a unique breed. They might have been wearing security badges and regulation uniforms, but they had natural flair. Their neck scarves were jauntily tied, their lipstick was bolder and their eyes more defined than what I was used to. They walked from the hip, the rolling, self-confident stroll of the born-to-it femme fatale. I will perfect this walk, I said to myself.

But at that moment my steps were hesitant. I had five years of high school French under my belt, but I was nowhere near being bilingual. I could conjugate verbs very well on paper, and I had a memory filled with French words. But coming from Toronto, where it was rare to hear any French spoken outside a classroom, I had little experience with the language in real time. I still struggled to piece sentences together to have a conversation. And so, in the airport, I walked in circles until I understood what door to exit from.

Adding to my confusion was my quest for a woman I had never met before. The plan was for me to stay with her in her apartment for a week, after which Jenna and Nigel were expected to arrive in Paris with their two sons. I would then move in with them in the large Left Bank apartment they had rented for July and August. I was told we would live there *en famille,* as a family, until I flew back to Toronto at the end of the summer to begin classes as a newbie undergraduate at the University of Toronto.

Without consulting me, Jenna had scheduled her arrival in Paris after mine, stranding me in a city where I knew no one. The woman I was meeting, my temporary chaperone, was a friend of a friend of a friend. I had only a name, but still I strained to look for her, which was stupid because I had no idea what she looked like.

Then I saw her: birdlike in her smallness, not chic like the Sirens I had seen just beyond the gate, but quirkier, with lank brown hair falling over an aubergine linen vest paired with a cream-colored, knee-length skirt and black leather high heels worn without stockings. In her hand was a sign with my name on it, written in the flowery French hand, the first letter drawn out so that it resembled a curving line of poetry.

I walked up to her and with a small cough said I believed I was the person she was looking for.

"Enchantée," she responded and held out a fragile arm. *"Je suis Yolande Thiolat."*

She didn't so much speak the words as sing them. The first part was low register, the second part high and melodic, like the ringing of bells. She smiled and with her thin hand shook mine. In an instant she made me feel not a burden but a guest.

She escorted me to her car, a minuscule egglike structure just perfect for a birdwoman like her. It was bent and
scratched beyond the ken of a North American like me
used to large buffed cars, and it was littered with old newspapers and magazines, for which she didn't apologize.
When she turned the key in the ignition, the radio wailed
an exotic tune. She lit a cigarette and asked if I'd like one.
"Non, merci," I said, as I craned my neck left and right so as
not to miss a single detail on the A3 expressway to Paris.

Yolande, I could see, was as shy as I was. She didn't
know any English, so I was forced to push through my
self-consciousness to communicate with her. My first name
she found impossible to pronounce. Deer-a-la? Drew-dree?
I told her to call me DiDi instead, if that would help. *"Bon!"*
She looked relieved. She asked me about the woman who
had brought us together, someone I didn't know at all, an
acquaintance of Jenna's back in Toronto. But to spare her
the complicated rehashing of how I ended up, a stranger, in
her car, I just said, *"Elle est ça va,* er, *très bien. J'espère."* She
was fine, I hoped.

Then suddenly, there it was: the Eiffel Tower. It didn't
need translating. I had seen this image—a skirted triangle crisscrossed with steel, a towering interjection, Paris
stretched between heaven and earth—a million times
before in pictures, on television, in travel books. But to
be confronted with the real thing? I couldn't believe it!

Yolande felt my enthusiasm and smiled generously as she emphatically pronounced the obvious, *"Ah, oui! La Tour Eiffel!"*

She lived in a tiny one-bedroom apartment, a cozy nest of a place, in the 19th Arrondissement. The neighborhood on the northern outreach of Paris had the feel of a village. Her building had at its doorstep a small café, a grocery store, a *boulangerie,* and a mechanics shop on the corner. There, men in blue overalls aired themselves out with talk and cigarettes and coffee drunk out of dainty white demitasse cups that shone against their blackened hands. Everyone greeted each other with a solemn *bonjour* and a nod of the head. These Old World manners had a certain archaic quality that immediately charmed me and made me feel I had broken through the looking glass. I was now dreamily on the other side, in a world made exotic by all these little differences between home and here.

Yolande had unrolled a mattress for me on the floor. I would sleep in her living room, which was about as big as a baby's carriage. The telephone was next to my head. French doors closed off the room from the hallway leading to her room. The closetlike toilet and a kitchen barely accommodating a round table lay just beyond my feet. Paris might sit big in the imagination, but in reality it is small, a city in which space is at a premium. I was taking it all in, my mind swimming in new thoughts and sensations.

Yolande asked if I was tired. I was. It was barely noon, but I was ready for bed. She left me alone, and I thought of my mother. In spite of everything, I loved her. Her face was before me as I blinked my eyes and fell asleep.

I DIDN'T WAKE up until almost twenty-four hours later. Rising the next day—my first Parisian morning!—I was greeted by Yolande, who had prepared a steaming bowl of café au lait for me, along with a wedge of leftover baguette that she had grilled in her oven and that she served with dollops of raspberry jam and butter. It was delicious. I reminded myself to wake like this every day, from now until death, amen.

I felt tongue-tied, but I had to speak; she was being so kind to me. I asked her about her work. She said she worked with a charitable organization, giving aid to people in Africa. She travelled sometimes, she said, rubbing her belly, which is how she met the father of her unborn child, an American whom she was supposed to marry in time for the baby's birth. I was taken aback. I hadn't realized.

They had met in some far-flung airport, both of them waiting for connecting flights: she to Paris, he to California, where he was from, and where she was expecting to move in a few months' time. She needed a visa first. He was going to call her today; would I help her, as her English was terrible?

I was overwhelmed by her story. I imagined her, frag-ile yet quirkily sexy, standing aloof in an airport lounge. I saw the locking of eyes with a complete stranger, the eruption of passion, the desire growing despite the distances. Wow. How French. She was not my guardian anymore. She was canvassing to be a friend. She took me by the arm and walked me around the quarter, talking all the time of *"amour."* She said we should take coffee, and I followed her through the doors of the neighborhood café.

Our café had a pinball machine in the corner, which irked me because it played the theme song from *Rocky* and I wanted to hear Édith Piaf. The coffee, however, lived up to my expectations. Black with a chocolate-brown foam on top, the aroma of old trees after a rain, the taste of a dark kiss of caramel—seductively addictive.

On the stroll back to her apartment I took in the lace curtains sashed like dresses, wooden shutters on every window, red geraniums in terra-cotta pots languishing in the sun, handbags worn crossed over the shoulder to rest on the opposite hip. I felt very happy.

Yolande's American lover called a few days later. I knew it was him when I heard Yolande gush into the phone, *"Ah, mon amour!"* I felt a certain thrill when I heard those words. It was like watching a French movie, but without subtitles. I was living a French love story vicariously. Yolande never stopped moaning and sounding kisses for her lover. The experience felt like a fur coat in July: very heavy, very hot, not a little suffocating. Suddenly Yolande grabbed me by the arm to take the receiver. She needed a translator. She really couldn't understand a word. And she was having his baby.

"I can't stop thinking of you," he said. His name was Dennis. I wanted to interrupt him, to let him know that I was on the line, but he kept going.

"Je rêve de toi—des rêves très sexy, bien sûr." He spoke terrible French.

"J'aime ton corps, tes yeux. Est-ce que tu rêves de moi?"

I tried giving the phone back to Yolande, but she pushed it back on me. I pushed it toward her again, and there we were, having a tug-of-war in her small apartment while her long-distance lover droned on.

She was mouthing for me to say something, and so I said, in a high-pitched voice that I thought sounded like Yolande's, *"Oui, je rêve de toi aussi."* Yes, I also dream of you.

There was silence on the other end.

"Yolande? Yolande?"

I panicked. I broke into English and said that Yolande was here and that I was her friend and that she loved him and that she was glad to be having his baby. *"Allô? Allô?"*

He thought that the transatlantic line had broken up and that he was now listening in on someone else's conversation. *"Yolande, c'est une mauvaise ligne,"* he said.

I told Yolande to say good-bye. She erupted into an aria of au revoirs and sent him countless air kisses that sounded like the broken chirps of a hungry bird. And then she hung up on him as he was still talking. We both sat on her living room floor looking at each other and at the phone, now silent, lifeless. She bit her lower lip, trying not to cry. She asked me if I wanted some tea. I nodded my head and got up to help. We moved without talking, bumping into each other in the confined space, both of us electrified by this long-distance love affair. I wondered if the baby was kicking yet.

A FEW DAYS later Yolande took me to Boulevard Saint-Germain, where Left Bank intellectuals like Jean-Paul Sartre and Simone de Beauvoir were then still living and working. We sat at one of their hangouts, Les Deux Magots, to watch the passersby. I knew of Les Deux Magots. It had also been the stomping ground of the American expats between the wars. Yolande reeled off their names: Hemingway, Fitzgerald, Pound. She had brought me there on purpose because she knew I would enjoy soaking up the ambience. We ordered white wine. She watered hers down with a Perrier. *"À cause du bébé."* I drank to that.

Inside the café many people sat alone nursing their café crèmes and quietly scowling at the day's newspaper headlines. Others hunched together in pairs or in groups of three or more—laughing and talking, exchanging ideas and sharing intimacies—people doing exactly as I had imagined people do in Paris, living life in the open, with passion and intensity. The chatter filled my ears as if it were a glorious symphony. A spoon clattered against the terrazzo floor. An old waiter tutted under his breath as he stopped to pick it up. A young couple was necking hungrily in a booth, their ardor reflected in the large wall mirrors that made the café perfect for people-watching. I took it all in, this throbbing spectacle of Parisian life. I understood why books had been conceived here, why the expats had made this their social club. Every character, every plot line was here. All you had to do was sit and look and engage.

A male friend of Yolande's waved to her as he walked past. It was a chance encounter, and Yolande, offering a chair for him to join us, introduced me as *"une amie."* That felt nice. I wasn't used to being called a friend. In Toronto I had been more of a loner, forced by necessity, by an inner imperative to succeed, not to bog myself down in intimate relationships. But in Paris I saw how enriching close, spontaneous encounters could be. And so we got talking, discussing the recent election of Margaret Thatcher, the right to strike, and the Americanization of French culture. I didn't notice at first how much I was talking and, to my astonishment, talking rapidly, in French, until we started walking, the three of us, him close to me, brushing against my arm—flirting? I wasn't sure. All I knew was that I liked the sensation, liked the effect these days in Paris were already having on me, making me feel confident, more alive than before. Proudly feminine. I was laughing and, incredible to me, they were laughing with me, at something amusing I had just said, and in a foreign language no less. A new me was being born, kicking free of her shell.

THAT FEELING OF spontaneous joy was short-lived. Jenna and Nigel and their children arrived two days later, and as I bade farewell to Yolande, who kissed me on both cheeks, I said good-bye to my burgeoning independence. I knew it the second I walked into their rooms, located in a rather dowdy hotel near the Notre-Dame-de-Lorette metro station, but within walking distance of the grand Boulevard Haussmann and its art nouveau department stores, Printemps and Galeries Lafayette. I had been buoyant, uplifted by *un bel esprit*. They were tired, cranky, not disposed to talking. Jenna said, "Nigel and I need to rest. You stay with the children." Then, "Here," as she threw me a towel. "Wash Edward. He's soiled himself." She went into a room across the hall and shut the door. I was disappointed at hearing English again—and English telling me to clean a little boy's bottom. I hoped it would get better. I was back at the beck and call of a mom. I didn't know if the children had eaten. I tapped lightly on her door.

"Yes?"

Entering the dimly lit room, I saw Jenna curled up like a cat in a chair. She had been reading a book and was wearing a white nightgown that fell over her scrawny frame, accentuating its bony thrusts and edges. With her large saucerlike eyes she looked at me expectantly.

"Yes?" she repeated.

I asked about dinner and she batted her thick black lashes. She had forgotten completely about it.

"Do be a darling," she said in that plummy English accent, more Oxonian than East London, where she had grown up as an Eastern European immigrant after the war, an upper-crust inflection acquired when her scientist husband had had a year-long sabbatical in Oxford around the time their first child had been born. "Go to the corner and buy us some salads."

Out in the Parisian streets in search of a charcuterie, I realized that Jenna had failed to give me any money. I worried that I might not have enough. But it was too late to go back now, empty-handed. I imagined her purr turning to a hiss, underscoring my incompetence. I thought it better to just get her fed, and so spent my last change on shaved carrots with mayonnaise, celery hearts with olives. When I returned, she had the kids gorging on crackers and chocolate bars shored up in her purse. She called that kind of eating "grazing" and thought it very anti-bourgeois, as she liked to tell me. She prided herself as a beautiful rebel. I stood with my beautifully wrapped takeout and gaped. I had been in Paris long enough to have forgotten how complicated and inscrutable she was.

I had met Jenna when I was fifteen, the night of her thirtieth birthday. Nigel, her sister, and her brother-in-law were waiting in the living room to take her to dinner. I had been hired to babysit Christopher, then six, and Edward, not yet one. Jenna had kept everyone waiting. Then she descended the staircase in flowing black velvet pants and a white silk blouse, tasteful and elegant. She relished the admiration of the audience gazing up at her from the bottom step. I soon learned that she always needed to be the center of attention. I certainly didn't deny her that; I thought she was wonderful, a woman of real sophistication. I had lived with her the first time I wanted to be away from my mother. My mother resented her for it and told me that Jenna was taking advantage of me, exploiting me as her domestic help—free housecleaning, free babysitting. But I didn't mind. I was Eliza Doolittle to her Henry Higgins.

"I've never had a daughter, and you can be her," she had said.

After that night, Jenna embarked on a mission to bring me up to her standard. A female Svengali, she brought me books that I had never heard of but that she was sure would help me become sophisticated. "You must introduce yourself to Justine," she would say, for instance. She meant the main female character in Lawrence Durrell's *The Alexandria Quartet*.

"After reading about her you will understand that if I had a daughter, I would name her Justine. In fact, you remind me of her, my darling DiDi." I strained to see myself in that dusky woman's quest for sexual liberation. The notion was quite stirring, since I was then just a pimply-faced adolescent.

Jenna's first line of business was to turn me into an aesthete. She told me my model would be Oscar Wilde and gave me his book of epigrams. I had never read anything like it. I had never before known intelligence to be so playful. Jenna pressed me to enjoy nuance and elliptical wit. Perhaps to please her, I became a Wilde devotee. I studied everything he wrote and read his biographies. I gave a presentation at my high school, addressing the class with a green carnation tucked into a red, vintage-store sweater. When I told my classmates the only thing separating me from art was a buttonhole—I was paraphrasing Wilde himself—they sat at their desks with their jaws open. One girl even cried. My highly flamboyant teacher rose in his chair, staring. He gave me the highest grade in the class.

In true Wildean fashion I became anticonformist. I wore men's ties to school. I bought vintage before it was cool— fluttery white camisoles, which I wore with a Laura Ashley skirt (bought on sale). I toyed with smoking after Jenna introduced me to colored cocktail cigarettes. I took them to Susan's house, and in her family's basement we took turns puffing on Turkish tobacco wrapped in paper-stained chartreuse and fuchsia, peacock and saffron. They had gold tips. God, we were swank.

Jenna had a high school teaching certificate but as yet no job. She never stopped reading, never tired of accumulating information. She would typically read and watch television at the same time, effortlessly absorbing ideas that she would then ruminate on out loud, drawing me into a seductive web of learning.

She and Nigel went on dates to listen to chamber ensembles. I used to think that was boring. Nigel said, "You only say that because you don't know." He was right. My musical taste until then included just about everything but classical music. I listened to Deep Purple, Pink Floyd, Genesis, the Beatles (in grade 7 I had changed my middle name from Lynne to Lennon), Led Zeppelin, Thin Lizzy, Supertramp, Queen, David Bowie, Lou Reed, Rick Derringer, and Bruce Springsteen. I embraced anything with a rebel yell.

Part of my rehabilitation at the book-lined Toronto home of Jenna and her behind-the-scenes husband was a steady exposure to classical music, in particular Dvořák's New World Symphony. Its lush orchestration resonated within me, inducing me, indeed, to enter a new world of aural stimulation. I was obviously an eager convert: within a few months I hawked my copy of *Ziggy Stardust* to younger students in our high school library. I dove into Stravinsky next. Jenna urged me to comment on what I heard.

If what I said sounded facile to her, she would say, "Oh, don't be so stupid. Think before you talk!" I accepted all her put-downs because I thought I needed to be pushed beyond the borders of my intellectually limited upbringing. I wanted sophistication and believed that she would give it to me.

I believed this even more strongly in Paris. Our ultimate destination in the city was a sprawling apartment on the Left Bank situated at number 26 Rue de l'Université, a stone's throw from the Louvre. I didn't realize it then, but it was a posh address, the domicile of aristocrats with no money. They went away for the summer, as all good Parisians do, but instead of leaving their place empty, they rented it out in order to afford their lifestyle in the south of France. It came furnished in a frumpy ancien régime style—sea-foam love seats with curlicue arms, ebony side tables with lion's feet, a marble fireplace strewn with ash and desiccated orange peels. But the one accessory none of us had expected was Luc, the family's heir, a skinny, earringed, blue-jeaned, hypercoifed would-be Baudelaire who for the first week or so could barely allow himself a terse *bonjour* when he strode, seminaked, into the kitchen to grill himself some toast.

He was exactly my age, I discovered, but he couldn't have been more different. He partied all night, slept until noon, spoke incessantly on the phone, smoked all the time, and was never without the season's item of cool—which at that moment happened to be pointy snakeskin cowboy boots. He could speak English fluently, and with a British accent (finishing school, no less), but he rarely spoke to me. Jenna and Nigel whispered behind his back that he was so rude! So French! They were convinced that he never bathed and, worse, that he was some kind of drug addict.

Look at the dark circles under his eyes! His suite of rooms was just beyond ours, separated by French doors that he sometimes left open. I could see him late in the afternoon slouched in an armchair intently reading a book. I assumed by the cover that it was real literature, and this intrigued me. French layabouts are different from you and me: they have a grand tradition to defend, ideas, books, art, late-night assignations. These are a Parisian's birthright.

I was strenuously not attracted to him. Still, I wanted him to recognize in me a similar yearning for adventure and fun. We were of the same generation. I had grown up in North America, thinking that meant something. I wondered why he never asked me to go to the nightclubs he bragged about after a night of revelling, sleep thick and yellow in the corners of his eyes. I wasn't ugly. Why did he brush me off? Why did he butter his toast in front of me in our crowded kitchen (and who had invited him?), with an insouciance bordering on disdain?

But then I found out. After a couple of weeks of him avoiding me, even as we brushed up against each other in the apartment's tight squeeze of a kitchen, I mentioned to him that I'd like to go dancing. That stopped him cold. Turning to me, he said, "The au pair does not go to the nightclubs."

I thought I would die.

It was Jenna's fault. She told him I was the au pair. Jenna hadn't ever said those words, au pair, to me. In Paris, I learned, the words au pair were equivalent to "servant." I was beneath an aristocrat's contempt.

Soon after that I started hearing the words au pair a lot. Jenna now felt comfortable in her new domain of Paris. In bookstores, where she would order me to carry her piles of hardcover purchases, she would wave her hand gaily in my direction and tell the strangers behind the counter that there I was, the au pair, the staff. Except that I wasn't being paid. That had been the arrangement. I paid my own way there, and in exchange for room and board I was to look after the children, which should be pleasant enough because I genuinely adored them. Jenna had called me a member of the family, the daughter she'd never had. She had promised me that I would see Paris, experience it like a local. She had never before used the words au pair. Tra-la-la-ing it in Paris, she waited to hear the stony-faced shopkeepers repeat au pair back to her, with as much enthusiasm as they might reserve for the word *merde*, or shit, with hardly a glance in my direction. I got the impression that I was supposed to just sink into the book-lined walls, disappear from view. I wished that I could.

Eventually Jenna barely spoke to me at all except to issue orders. I had beds to make, floors to sweep, dishes to wash, baguettes to buy—before she woke up in the morning. One day she wrote the house rules on a piece of paper. I had a half-day off during the week to EXPLORE PARIS ON

YOUR OWN. Those were her capital letters, not mine. I cleaned in desultory silence. I didn't know what I had done wrong. But I wanted desperately to make things right.

I went out later that day, alone, a copy of *A Moveable Feast* in hand (Jenna had dismissed Anaïs Nin as being all wrong for my Paris education), feeling very lonely as I attempted to retrace Hemingway's steps through the city. I had no one my age to talk to. My mother was an expensive long-distance call away, and, anyway, what would she say other than I told you so? She hated Jenna, hated her for taking me away from her—which was how she put it, but it was more that my mother had driven me into the arms of another mother, one who was more cultured.

For a long while I sat by the Medici fountain in the Jardin du Luxembourg. The waters were as deep and dark as my mood. It was quickly becoming become my favorite place in Paris—away from the crowds, the laughing faces, that now seemed to mock my ineptitude.

The fountain was in a long shallow pool that stretched out before a sculpture showing Polyphemus, a cyclops in Greek mythology, spying from an overhead perch on the young lovers Actis and Galatea. It was tucked into a corner of the gardens, bordered by elegant stone urns containing brightly colored flowers whose reflection danced on the water. No one ever seemed to go there. It was hidden, romantic, soothing, its beauty heavy and melancholy. It felt perfect for the person I was that summer in Paris. What I really wanted was to be accepted for myself, but I didn't have that insight, yet.

I spied a *fleuriste* and bought some paperwhites, or white narcissi, for Jenna. I had always bought presents for my own mother, even when (or was it because?) she behaved callously toward me.

When I arrived back at the apartment, I knocked at the door instead of walking straight in. Jenna answered and I pushed the flowers toward her and said, *"Ça ne fait rien"* (it doesn't matter), a phrase I had learned in high school and had rehearsed that day in my mind, thinking it would endear me to her. I hoped she would think me clever. She listened to me, looking at me as if I were daft. She had that perfect hostess face on, the one with the magnanimous smile and the blank eyes. Her prolonged silence said to me, "You are a complete imbecile."

Looking bemused at the proffered bouquet, Jenna purred, "Oh, they're lovely." She flashed a smile like scissors, little white teeth cutting a look of irony into her face. I felt so defeated. I had never understood sophistication to be mean, but it is. If you look up the origin of the word (something Jenna would have approved of), there you find it—a hardening of innocence. My own process of becoming sophisticated could not have happened in a more appropriate place than Paris. A center of enlightenment for centuries, it was where countless people before me had come to get the bumpkin kicked out of them. Paris was my salon, with Jenna playing hostess. She was exacting, reproving me every time I fell short of the Paris ideal of the smart, refined, artfully cunning female.

Under such stress, much of it self-imposed, an anxiety born of the need to be more than perfect around such apparently faultless people as Jenna and Nigel, every corner of Paris seemed to taunt me with images of sublime perfection—the *Arc de Triomphe,* the Champs-Élysées, Napoleon's tomb ensconced under the golden cupola of Les Invalides, the futuristic Centre Pompidou with its building's guts hanging on the outside. Even the art began to weigh me down, as I discovered the afternoon I visited the atelier of the French Romantic painter Eugène Delacroix, located on the tiny Place Furstenberg, down the street from the apartment. It had been his residence, and studies for his enormous canvasses now hanging in the Louvre were on display. But even though these preliminary paintings were smaller, they were just as magnificent and decadent as the final paintings, each dripping with blood and morbid sensuality. They intimidated me, made me feel small, made me feel acutely my own mortality, and I was just nineteen.

MY LAST SIX and a half weeks in Paris were one long and inglorious existential moment. I should have been enjoying myself, should have been relishing my first time in Paris as a young woman. This was the capital of feminine charm! But instead I too often worried about doing and saying the right things. I felt this mostly when confined to the apartment, with its strange ménage à trois brewing inside its stuffy rooms. Outside that oppressive apartment I liked my relationship with Paris. I pursued a growing relationship with the city itself. I found that if I let it, Paris could seduce me, make me feel alluring. At the Louvre one day a young Parisian in a dress shirt and tailored pants, blonde hair combed back and smelling of an expensive woodsy cologne, cruised me while I was eyeing the *Grande Odalisque* by the French painter Ingres. He invited me, at the instant, to run away with him to his family château in the country. I didn't go, of course. But inwardly I wanted to abandon all responsibility, embrace what he was obviously embracing: a vision of me as desirable.

My only real companions in Paris were the two boys under age ten whom I was there to mind. They were also my only hope of feeling I was good at something. I was, if nothing else, a gifted babysitter. I loved children. As a teenager I had happily volunteered at the Catholic Children's Aid in the newborn division.

I took both children to the Jardin du Luxembourg, where there were swings and a sandbox—a real park by Canadian standards. That was where the other children of Paris were—never scattered in the street but enclosed in leafy green spaces where you could admire them, as you did the outdoor sculpture ringing the periphery. I stood by, watching little girls in starched white dresses, patent shoes, and ribbons in their neatly plaited hair, little boys in seersucker shorts, knee socks, and handsome cotton vests worn over their linen short-sleeved shirts. As they ran up and down the ladder of stairs connected to the slide, stern-faced adults supervising their every move (and quick to shove their charges into sweaters at even a suggestion of a sneeze), I wondered why Parisians ritualized child's play, kept it in a special place. My mother let my brother, Kevin, and me play outside for hours and we always knew to return home at dusk.

Jenna and Nigel raised their children differently. They were always supervised; there was an understanding that these children were to be intellectually guided every step of their young lives. But when I was out of Jenna and Nigel's sight, I let the children run wild. I forbade them to read out of doors. I dressed them in T-shirts and shorts. They were a stark contrast to the French kids, perfectly pressed and in linen. We looked like vagabonds, loitering around the large fountain pools, making smacking noises at the large gold carp swimming brightly beneath the surface. Christopher once threw a handful of sand into the pool, eliciting stares and hissing sounds. I pretended I didn't hear. Later in the evenings, as was the house rule, I slept with the children in their room. Edward kicked me in the belly. Christopher lay wrapped tightly in his dreams, holding my hand. I felt at times they were my children, and because of them I vowed, once I grew up, to have a house full of boys for myself.

I wrote my mother impassioned words on picture post-cards of Paris, feigning delight in my new surroundings. But my messages inevitably ended with, "Wish you were here." I meant it. I wanted to share with her what I was experiencing, not the angst, but the aching beauty of the place.

The Paris gardens were graceful oases of picturesque charm, open at all times to the public and punctuated by an obelisk or a decorative arch or the visual folly of a fountain that made its waters perform arabesques against a serge-blue sky. There were always chairs scattered about—thin and made of faded wrought iron. No one ever stole them, it seemed, or dirtied them with graffiti. People seemed to respect that the chairs were there for their enjoyment. And they looked as if they did enjoy them, taking for granted, I sometimes thought, their city's largesse. Paris exalted people with all sorts of sensual gifts. This wasn't true of all cities, certainly not my own city of Toronto, where chairs, if they were made available at all to the public, would be bolted down and made of ugly prison-issue concrete. Toronto underscored that people were inherently bad, not to be trusted, while Paris, embracing a Rousseauian point of view, allowed that people, whether rich or poor, were good and deserving of all the fine things in life, like a pretty garden view.

I thought everyone should see Paris, if just once. Paris galvanizes you, makes you think of better things, be a better person. I wanted my mother to partake in that, to grow as well. Grow with me, not against me. Grow closer.

But she was about as good a writer as she was a reader. The one letter I received from her, almost at the end of my trip, ignored my veiled screams for help. She wrote, "Hi there. Having an okay summer. Some rain. Mother."

In the meantime I felt as if I were sinking in mud. My shoulder-length hair lacked the bounce and shine of the hair belonging to other young women I saw in Paris that summer, whom I also envied for their apparent nonchalance, the ease of living well inside their own skins.

Certainly they exuded confidence, and even if they weren't beautiful their belief in themselves made them so. They plucked their eyebrows to frame their expressive eyes and were never seen without lipstick—pink for day, red for night. They wore heels with their jeans and walked with heads held high, miraculously avoiding the dog poop that clotted the city's sidewalks. Their earrings were small and discreet, pearls or small gold hoops. Ostentation they left to the North American women who, during a gathering of the crowds at the Place de la Concorde on Bastille Day, stood out for wearing garish T-shirts instead of starched blouses, rumpled shorts instead of sleek skirts. French women were all pencil thin. I furtively watched them in the cafés, eating salade niçoise and drinking red wine. When they exited, they walked tall, and their hair fell coyly over their shoulders. No au pairs here. I felt that my hair constantly betrayed me by underscoring how hopelessly unchic I was. It was my dunce's cap, my beanie of defeat.

And my clothes! I had a suitcase full of hand-me-downs from one of my girlfriends, who had generously given them to me on the occasion of my trip abroad. All wrong! They were several sizes too big, and besides, embroidered granny dresses were not my style or the prevailing style of Paris. I felt ragged in these second-hand clothes. I really was the au pair, living off the avails of others. But I was in no position to complain. I had no real wardrobe of my own.

My situation was complicated by a food fetish that had flowered in Paris, city of sybaritic pleasures. I thought that if I could only be thin enough, no one would notice what a North American oaf I was. I wanted to shrink from scrutiny and the burden of feeling that I wasn't good enough.

The irony was that we were all in Paris to make sure that Jenna got fat. She was certifiably anorexic. Her doctor had told her not to come back to Canada unless she gained at least ten to twenty pounds. And so she was on a mission to eat all the ice cream she could stomach. I watched from the sidelines, my arms tightly wrapped around my body, my fingers furtively counting every rib.

We were, consequently, all expected to eat fattening foods—*frites, crêpes aux marrons,* Brie on baguettes, mayonnaise with everything. Such a diet made me quite thin, almost as emaciated as Jenna, which is probably what I wanted, as subconsciously I wanted to be like her. I couldn't eat this food. It would make me fat, and fat to me was letting go, giving up control. And so I subsisted on *omelettes nature*, undressed eggs, with unbuttered bread. For dessert I once ordered an orange (it was on the menu), and Jenna hissed at me to cut it with a fork and knife. She watched, steely, as I tried to carve it into eight perfect bite-sized pieces. I ended up squirting both of us in the eye. From that day on, even fruit in Paris became a challenge for me.

One night when I was feeling oppressed by the coldness in the apartment, I decided to go for a walk through Saint-Germain in the dark. As I walked down the streets where Joyce had wandered half blind—he had once lived in the neighborhood—I became aware of the Friday-night crowd, consumed by a voluble joy. Their joviality startled me; I had become so used to gloom. Out of nowhere a man started walking next to me, speaking to me charmingly in French, a proposition to drink with him, I think, to share in the beauty of the night. His advances terrified me. I was like a bug under a stone suddenly exposed to the assault of daylight, and I squirmed and looked left and right for a place to scurry away to, to flee. It was an unexpected response. The poor man became alarmed and in the most polite of terms begged my forgiveness. He gave me a tiny bow and walked away. He probably thought I was mad.

I went to a coiffeuse to get my hair cut and styled. After I returned to our borrowed apartment, I saw myself in the large Louis xv mirror in Luc's sitting room; I can't recall why I was in there. But Luc didn't comment on my new, chic look. Nigel noticed, however, and said, "Have you done something with your hair?" I froze. I waited for a compliment to follow, prayed there would be one. "Pretty," he said. That's when I caught my reflection. I looked at myself, hard. Yes, pretty. For a day.

Jenna took me to the Rodin museum, where, like Miss Jean Brodie with one of her kilted schoolgirls, she educated me on the fecund possibilities of art. "Look at the thrust and curl of the body."

It was a tiny carving, entitled *A Dryad and a Faun*, and it depicted two nude forms in an arabesque of desire. I wanted to reach out and caress the marble, so smooth and sensually inviting. As Jenna said, there was raw sexual energy pulsating just beneath the surface of the polished stone.

She moved on to the next in a series of amorous couplings. I stared, transfixed, at one carving that showed a male penetrating a female with such force that the ramrod form of the penis could be seen jutting out in the flesh on the female's back. "I'm getting horny," Jenna said. Her words shocked me. I was amazed that such smut could come out of such a supercilious mouth. I was also discombobulated by her response to the art, all wrong, of course, according to what I had learned in high school: art that excites feelings of desire in us is improper. Surely Jenna knew this Aristotelian rule of aesthetics?

I thought to say something, assert my knowledge. I coughed. Jenna laughed. She called me a prude.

"Oh, you're a lot of work."

She said it in a way that sounded affectionate, like I was a pet cause. I nodded in agreement. I had much to learn. I knew nothing of sexual freedom. I was afraid to fall. Art had been sheltering me from libidinous sin, and here was Jenna, of all people, tearing down the walls, exposing me to the elements of my own fears and apprehensions. So maybe she was a good teacher after all.

I left the museum that day without declaring the stirring of my loins but deciding to loosen my sense of decorum, which was outmoded and too old for my age anyway. Art was vital—I knew that—but in more ways than I had allowed.

It was during rare moments like these, with Jenna guiding me toward new pools of knowledge, that I was deliriously happy to be in Paris. I never wanted to leave. Despite the bitter taste of some of the medicine being forced down my throat, I felt that the experience was good for me, good for my post-adolescent soul in its quest for new sensations. That was the fantasy. Reality inevitably followed.

Jenna and Nigel had conspiratorially befriended Luc, unbeknownst to me. He was now sitting with us at the dinner table, talking with them, ignoring me. One day he invited the family to accompany him on a day trip to the Château de Vaux-le-Vicomte, near the village of Maincy in the region Seine-et-Marne, less than an hour's drive from Paris. As the children were included, I had to come along. There, on Luc's gill-gray skin, I noted a sudden blush of excitement brought on by the aristocratic grandeur of the 17th-century architecture. Or was it the middle-aged coquette holding onto his arm with all the put-on frail charm of a Marie Antoinette?

The largest château of its time—Vaux-le-Vicomte was the precursor to Versailles—the house that Nicolas Fouquet built was so daringly opulent that it drew the ire of Louis XIV and sealed his former finance minister's fate. The King himself was at Vaux-le-Vicomte on August 17, 1661, the night Fouquet hosted the debut of Molière's ironically named *Les Fâcheux* (The Angry).

Once the curtain had fallen on the play, Fouquet lit up the night sky with a spectacular fireworks display that shone unnatural light over his stately gardens with their cone-shaped trees and spiralling hedges that looked as if traced by a giant Spirograph. It was his final moment of glory.

Louis, suspecting that Fouquet had stolen public money to fund such a home and furious to have been upstaged by a member of his own staff, immediately had Fouquet arrested and eventually jailed him for life in the fortress at Pignerol. Fouquet died there twenty years later.

It was one of those stories of Paris's past that made my skin crawl. Violence lies always just below the city's surface beauty; betrayals, beheadings, blood running like water down the cobbled streets. That brutality was palpable still in the texture of everyday Parisian life—the aggressive driving, the bumper-car parking practices, the general rudeness of strangers when you, a tourist, asked for a direction. *"Là-bas,"* over there. Anything you were ever looking for in Paris was always, coldly, "over there."

Luc took us on a tour of the château, since restored to Fouquet's splendorous taste by the present owners, who actually lived on the premises but were far from sight, at least on that day. We strolled through rooms with chandeliers hanging from ceilings that were covered with painted images in gilt frames. We marvelled at the black-and-white marble floor and at the tall, arched windows that once shone light on the moral philosopher Voltaire as he lectured Fouquet's illustrious guests (no doubt on the folly of hubris) while leaning, perhaps, on the rose-red quartz table mounted by a massive bronze statue depicting hounds savaging a stag.

Afterward, Luc led us deep down into the dungeon, where I imagined Fouquet had probably been first imprisoned, still in his party clothes. The lighting was dim. The stone walls felt damp and cold. We were feeling our way into the gloom, waiting for our eyes to adjust to the blanketing darkness. At that moment Jenna tripped over a stone in the floor and fell. Luc dove at her feet.

He bent to pick her up. He was almost as scrawny as she was, but he was ready to carry her, Prince Charming–like, into the sunshine, to revive her among the roses. The scene made me want to puke.

Back at the Paris apartment, the intimacy thickened at dinner. The meal consisted largely of a single boiled artichoke naked on a large white plate with a small bowl of melted butter at the side. The four of us sat at the dinner table that could easily have accommodated sixteen. We were spread out around the table, with large spaces between us, like points on a compass. I had never eaten an artichoke before. Jenna, Nigel, and Luc were connoisseurs, and almost in unison they each plucked a leaf from atop the topiary-shaped vegetable and, after delicately dipping it in the sauce, clenched down with gritted teeth to scrape off a sliver of flesh.

I watched carefully. I would have to follow their lead if I wanted any dinner, and I would have to make sure I didn't commit some kind of faux pas lest they mock me some more. I took a leaf and put it in my mouth. It was spiky. I made a face. Jenna pretended not to notice. Luc smothered a laugh. Oh. I see. I am not supposed to eat the whole thing. I spat it out. Shrugged, self-deprecatingly. Soldiered on. We were all of us doing the artichoke striptease, one leaf at a time, round and round the rotund body, penetrating to the heart.

"How sensuous," Jenna said. Luc moaned in agreement. I looked at Nigel. Shouldn't he do something? He seemed to be locked inside some kind of inner monologue concerning an obscure philosophy. I was startled to find inside the plant a bearded center protecting the delicacy within. I commented that it looked like a walrus. Jenna said, "It's a vagina, darling. It's why the artichoke is the most glorious of aphrodisiacs." She looked at Luc, a captive audience of one. He applauded her wit. Jenna delighted in being outré, especially at my expense. I plucked at the grizzled bush until I exposed the heart. With one bite I discovered what all the fuss was about. It was tender as a petal, velvety soft and delicate, a taste like spring rain. Jenna was delighted.

"You see, Luc, she isn't without promise."

"But Zhennah," said Luc. "She ez too thin."

They were speaking as if I weren't there.

"In Frahnce we like our women not to be too thin. But you, Zhennah, you are pur-fect."

That was it. I threw my napkin onto the table and stormed off to sulk inside the laundry room, the only place I could have some privacy, but not before—and it even shocked me—I uttered the word "assholes" under my breath but loud enough for all to hear. I was sick of being humiliated because someone else needed to feel superior. It was my one moment of rebellion.

Jenna demanded that I return to the table, and in the most galling way told me to apologize to Luc for my rudeness. I was seething now. I wanted to run away. But I had no money of my own and nowhere to go. I was the au pair, indentured for the rest of my stay in Paris, forced to eat not artichoke anymore, but crow.

I returned, anger making my backbone ramrod straight, and in imitation of *Zhennah*, proclaimed in a flowery voice dripping with sarcasm, *Je m'excuse.*

Luc loved it. A few days later he asked for me to go out with him, without Jenna or Nigel. It was a luncheon date in the country with a married couple, friends of his, Mireille and Claude. The destination was Chantilly, the town renowned for its lace, where many great feasts had been consumed at the behest of General Condé, chief courtier of Louis XIV. What was it with Luc and the Sun King?

Condé's legacy had inspired the establishment of a five-star restaurant that on Sunday afternoons attracted Parisians in search of the religion of food.

Called the Table des Lions and located inside the old *fourrière*, a walled compound where carriages used to be housed, it was close to the Chantilly forest and château, a hunting retreat at the time of Louis XIV. It attracted a well-heeled crowd. Everyone was dressed in country chic—silk scarves tied just so and well-cut blazers worn with tight but impeccably pressed jeans. As in most French dining establishments I had so far visited that summer, the talk was as thick as the cloud of blue cigarette smoke that hung in the air. The dark wood interior was offset by white linen tablecloths that supported settings of silverware that to me seemed dauntingly French—four forks and an equal number of knives, several differently sized spoons including one as big as a gourd. I observed quietly, wondering how I would tackle it all. I decided to let Luc lead the way. I discovered that day that he was something of a connoisseur, which surprised me, considering that he always looked underfed.

I thought that by taking me there he was offering me a peace pipe of sorts, and I probably tried a little too hard to show that I was grateful. I laughed at his pale jokes. I took a cigarette when he offered one. I looked enraptured by a conversation involving truffles. Luc's friends—she a pharmacist, he a banker—were enthusiastic gourmands who wanted to identify every ingredient of every mouthful of food. I remember thinking how boring they were, how silly. Still, I played along. I drank the wine appreciatively and, when asked to describe the flavors dancing on my tongue, I said, a little whimsically, that I could taste chocolate and pale blue robin's eggs. Everyone at the table laughed. It felt good to be away from my keepers.

But even away from Paris, I wasn't free of its oppressive influence.

There had been several courses—herrings marinated in oil followed by a rabbit in white wine and a veal marengo served with stuffed baked potatoes, peas with bacon, and lettuce. There was strawberry charlotte for dessert and an upside-down apple cake served with eau de vie and black coffee. I thought it was over. Five hours had passed. And then the cheese trolley rolled our way, boasting dozens of choices—*Camembert, Gruyère, Roquefort, Brie.* Luc lifted a spoonful of a creamed cheese with berries that he wanted to put in my mouth. I guessed that all the rules had changed. He said, "You must eat." I declined, saying innocently enough, "I am full."

Zut! Catastrophe!

Luc put down the spoon, the smallest one. He leaned in to me and whispered, "In Frahnce it is *impoli* to say that, I'm full. It is *une gaucherie.* You understand?" I understood.

"You never say, I am full. You say *non, merci.* You politely decline."

He left the table, ostensibly to wash his hands. His words had smarted.

Later, when we went to the château where Condé had feted legions of guests, I heard the story of his chef who had committed suicide when the fish arrived late at a banquet. I felt his pain. I would have liked to kill myself then and there for being a social embarrassment. In Paris it seemed I would always be on the outside looking in. No matter how much I wanted the city to embrace me, it would always keep me at arm's length while wagging a finger in my face. I had rarely felt that I fit in—at home, at school, among my peers. But in Paris that feeling of alienation intensified. I didn't belong there, either. I shuffled back into my life as the au pair, taking the children to the park to play on the swings, playing hide-and-seek amid the statuary of gods, goddesses, nymphs, satyrs, dukes, duchesses, playwrights, painters, and other assorted heroes and heroines dotting the Paris landscape.

A WEEK LATER, we moved away from the Rue de l'Université apartment with its inner courtyard and ever-vigilant concierge, its arched and gated entranceway and elegant stone facade. Luc's parents were due back from the sunny south, and we had to move to less spacious and less central digs. We had been faux aristocrats in that rented eight-room apartment. Overnight we reentered the ranks of the proletariat, with four dingy rooms walled in by the rude noise of the incessant street traffic. The new apartment was across town in the nondescript 10th Arondissement, on the Right Bank, no less, far from anything beautiful or historically edifying, a district so blandly practical it was home to two railway stations—Gare du Nord and Gare de l'Est.

The assault on our sensibilities was almost too much.

Nigel, for one, responded by slapping one of his energetic and lively boys across the face so hard it made the boy's nose bleed. Such a sudden decline in standards made Paris seem even more brutal than before.

Luc should have stayed with the apartment we'd left, but there he was, helping the fragile Jenna carry her books up the new stairs. "It's just for a while, *cher* Luc. Until we get properly settled."

He understood reversals of fortune. It was why, I soon discovered, he was still part of our nomadic scene. I also understood the surge of interest in us, in me. He was crafting a connection to North America, a bridge of opportunity.

Unbeknownst to me, Jenna had been talking up her brother-in-law, Colin, proprietor of a successful auction house in Toronto that had a cache of rich clients attached to it. The rooms of Ross Galleries were stacked with fine furniture and objets d'art, exactly the kind of place in which an unemployed Parisian with a sense of entitlement could feel at home. When Luc heard "auction house," he doubtless thought Sotheby's or Christie's. Ross was nowhere in that league. But it was an in, of sorts, and a way to explore the New World in a manner Luc had grown accustomed to—surrounded by beauty and sensual charm.

To make sure that I might be of some use to him in the near future, toward my final days in Paris, Luc, out of nowhere, proposed to show me Paris by night on the back of a motorbike. Since Chantilly I had been keeping my distance. But this sounded like fun. And I didn't have to talk to him, risk embarrassing myself again. I just had to hold on and enjoy the ride.

He knew the city, knew where the crowds were and weren't on this late summer night. We roared down main boulevards, almost wiping out whole families, and then bumped down cobblestone streets where there was hardly a person. Paris was mesmerizing at midnight. The lights shone bright through the darkness, velvet lozenges of blurred color, and because I was sitting and watching the scenery whiz by, I got a sense of the city as a panoramic spectacle, dramatic even without the interaction of people. The city's monumentality was the main event.

I clung to Luc, held tightly to his waist as he whipped around corners and the wind licked my hair. It didn't matter that it was dishevelled now. I was, belatedly, enjoying myself.

We motored past a café that looked as if it had been painted by Van Gogh. I felt a wave of nostalgia in anticipation of the moment, a few days hence, when I would have to leave this place and all its memories, victories, and defeats. Luc put his foot to the gas. We lurched ahead. I wanted to linger over my reverie, but he stopped in front of a building and said, "Let's go up."

It was a friend's apartment, but the friend wasn't there. Luc had a key, however. I supposed this was the communal sex pad, where young French aristos came when they wanted to get laid and their parents were at home. A *garçonnière*. Luc sat on the floor in his faded designer jeans, the toes of his cowboy boots worn and dirty, and rolled a joint. He asked did I want some? It just wasn't my thing. But I knew to say, *"Non, merci."* He smiled. Then he inhaled.

He closed his eyes. In a moment he was asleep, and there I was in a strange apartment with an even stranger young man. Who had bad manners now? I let him sleep for about thirty minutes. Then I woke him with a gentle kick. *"On y va,"* I said. Let's go. He smiled sheepishly. I helped him up. We didn't speak on the way back. Couldn't. The wind was in our ears and our mouths. Then again, there was nothing more to say.

I FOLLOWED A different flight path home. I stopped first in Newfoundland and then changed planes for a direct flight to Toronto. After two months in Paris, city of chic, I gazed despondently at the assembly of my fellow Canadians—a dowdy lot, dressed in cutoffs and T-shirts, without any discernible sense of style. I was reminded of how uninspiring I found my native land.

My mother was waiting for me at the airport. We embraced. I was happy to see her, yet sad too. I had returned with books and postcards and stories of all that I had seen and done, silk scarves and perfumes as presents, and emboldened ambition.

She spoke to me about the neighbor's dog barking through the night, the fact that my brother was in trouble again, that it had rained and then it had been hot. All the flowers had died. I had returned home to a lunar landscape. I sat next to her in the car in silence. Nothing had changed. Except for me.

I realized in that moment that I had grown even more determined to transcend the narrow confines of my life in southern Ontario. I would return to Paris—but next time on my own terms and better prepared for the challenge. I was about to start my university education and saw it as a means to an end, the goal being freedom and happiness in the most beautiful city on earth.

Although I had secured an entrance scholarship to the university, I still needed some money to help me get by. Within a few days of my return I went from the glory of the *Arc de Triomphe* to the whitewashed arches of Toronto's Princess Gates, entryway to the Canadian National Exhibition, a horse-and-cow event stinking of sweat, candy floss, and manure. I landed a last-minute job on the midway, convincing passersby to divest themselves of seventy-five cents to toss beanbags into a boxed set of squares in order to win a stuffed animal. "Don't walk by until you've given it a try."

This was my cri de coeur in the final days of the summer of 1979, my last days as an adolescent. My last days at home.

TWO

Wannabe

· 1983 ·

I BOUGHT MY plane ticket with some of the money I had won for making the principal's list in my final weeks as an undergrad. The funds were earmarked for graduate school, Plan B in case my dream of becoming a writer in Paris didn't pan out. I had been accepted to start the master's program in the fall, which was my mother's idea. She had originally wanted me to be a lawyer. A more practical and rewarding career than writing. But for the last four years I had been writing for the student newspapers, and when my mother saw my name in print, she started to come around to liking the idea of me becoming a journalist. When I took her along with me to some of the shows I was then reviewing as a fledgling dance critic, we'd sit in the best seats and be fawned upon at intermission by publicists and impresarios. She liked that, the idea of me getting attention, as she imagined some of it reflecting on her. But since I was to be a writer, she wanted me to stand head and shoulders above the pack. It's why she insisted I get the postgraduate degree. "To show that you are a cut above, which you are," she said. "We both are."

But I knew I wouldn't do it. By that September I expected to be properly ensconced in Paris, with a job. I didn't tell my mother that. I didn't tell anyone. I just told her that I was going to Paris for the summer, to spend time with an old high school friend, Danielle, who had offered me a bed to sleep in for a few weeks until another one of her Toronto friends arrived in June. My mother said, "Go, have a good time. You deserve it. You've worked so hard." And so in May of 1983, after writing my final exams, I sailed out of the ivory tower on fairy wings. I was free and ready for adventure, for all that might involve. On the plane ride over I wrote out a to-do list. Right after Get Job I wrote Get Boyfriend. The blank space that followed filled me with fear and longing.

For the trip, my mother had bought me a pair of red ballerina flats, a nod to my dance obsession. I wore the shoes as soon as I got to Paris, where it rained incessantly. I stepped in puddles everywhere. Soon my new shoes started to disintegrate, staining my feet crimson. As they peeled away in my hands, I saw that they were made of cardboard, which I was sure my mother hadn't known when buying them. She probably got them cheap. But she had meant well, and so I never told her how the shoes had turned my feet red as blood. Besides, that spring the 1948 film *The Red Shoes* was playing regularly at a cinema near the Place de l'Opéra. Set in Paris, it is about a dancer who can't stop dancing. With my stained feet, I saw myself cast in a similar role, partnered with Paris until I dropped. Even later, when back to wearing my old tennis shoes, the new red shoes tossed to the garbage, I continued to walk through Paris feeling connected to the city on a deeply emotional level. Despite the gloomy weather, in Paris I felt my senses awakening as if from a deep sleep. The city was a powerful stimulant that made me feel deliriously vibrant, invigorated, alive. The mighty Seine with its vaulting bridges, the narrow winding streets, the boutique windows showcasing the latest fashions, the mad swirl of traffic, was paradise to me. I felt a sense of inner joy. I felt I had come home.

Danielle had come to the airport to pick me up, but I barely recognized her. When I had last seen her, during our final year of high school four years earlier, she had been fat and dowdy. She had worn running shoes and jeans and, in the winter, snowflake sweaters buttoned up to her dimpled chin. She was a fashion disaster, but smart, with piercing blue eyes that sliced straight through you. But who was that swinging a black handbag at the turnstile? I recognized her by her laughter, a sound like wind chimes. She enveloped me with braceleted arms and kissed me twice, just like a Frenchwoman. It wasn't the only sign that since moving to Paris as an international business student a few years earlier, she had changed. She had never been a beauty. But Paris had somehow buffed her to a shine. She glowed from the inside out. While no less round, her fleshiness now appeared sleek and sophisticated. Clothes of a dramatic cut and color had replaced the ragtag wardrobe of old. On her lobes were discs of shining metal, the work of a local artisan. She had tamed her adolescent curls into a becoming style that encircled her face, enhancing the brilliance of her eyes. She had become a *parisienne*. I had always wanted to become one too, ever since encountering this rare breed on my first trip to Paris four years earlier. But back in Toronto I had fumbled in tying a silk scarf around my neck. I kohled my eyes, but the inky makeup made me look sick, not sleek. To be a member of this stylish breed, I thought you had to be born in Paris. But one look at Danielle and I could see that you just had to be open to the influence of Paris to make it happen. In a relatively short time Danielle had learned to walk the high-heeled walk. She possessed a poise that would have forever eluded her in flat-footed Toronto. I stared at her in amazement. If she could do it, become a woman of the world, then presto! so could I.

But she had an important advantage: family connections. Her aunt and uncle owned a flat at 27 Rue de Fleurus, in the same building where Gertrude Stein and Alice B. Toklas had famously hosted their literary salon. She held the keys to the garret on top of the family apartment, a former *chambre de bonne,* or maid's room, with a sharply slanted ceiling and a bird's-eye view of the rooftops of Paris. Danielle constantly mentioned this. It lent her cachet. She had lived there herself when she first moved to Paris almost five years earlier, before landing her job at a major French cosmetics company as a financial consultant. She had since moved on to more spacious digs in the up-and-coming Marais. But at that time she was in the habit of inviting deserving artists to live there in exchange for modest rent, and the promise of their company. Too practical to live hand to mouth herself, Danielle derived a vicarious thrill from befriending people committed to the bohemian ideal, mostly foreigners, as I was to discover.

One of them was an aspirant writer, also from Canada, whom Danielle had met months earlier through friends of friends. Tom, from rural Ontario, was firmly ensconced in the garret, "With no intention of leaving any time soon," Danielle said. "But I'll introduce you. Maybe he'll be useful."

We cut through the Jardin du Luxembourg, watching the puddles as we walked arm-in-arm toward the building that I had known since my high school days as a sanctuary for artists, having read *The Autobiography of Alice B. Toklas*. Danielle keyed in the access code on a panel located on an outside wall. I heard a click, and then together we pushed open the large glass doors covered with scrolling, black wrought iron. Huffing and puffing up five flights of stairs, we entered a narrow corridor with a number of small doors. Danielle stood before one of them, and knocked.

Tom didn't have a telephone and so hadn't been expecting us. He opened the door and blinked rapidly when looking into Danielle's smiling face, as if it were the first time he had seen anything brightly optimistic in days. Danielle introduced me, calling me her other writer friend. Tom had fine, wheat-colored hair and a sickly pale complexion. He extended his hand, lined with dark blue veins. His handshake was flaccid, his gaze indirect. He smelled of nicotine and wasted ambition. He asked us to come in. Spartan and small, with just a bed and a desk tucked under the window, the room had a beamed ceiling so low I had to duck when I entered. It reminded me of the student dormitory I had just escaped in Toronto, except it had a much better view. Beyond the curtainless window the rooftops of Paris undulated against a purple-and-pink sky. I looked out at the city spread beneath my feet and felt as buoyant as the birds. If I lived there, I thought, I would never lack for poetic inspiration.

Tom didn't have much to offer us. He didn't have a kitchen. But he had a pack of gum and offered us each a stick. I quietly chewed while Danielle asked him how things were going. He was writing a novel, he boasted. But it was tough going. He was twenty-nine, and whined that he was about to enter his thirties with nothing much to show for it. It was why he was in Paris. "If I don't write this book, I'll never be able to look at myself in the mirror." Paris, he said, would make him or break him.

I returned to Rue de Fleurus many times in the days that followed, calling on Tom to go for a coffee. Not that I liked him much. But Danielle worked during the day, and I was often alone, and being alone in Paris is not the happiest of circumstances. City of alienation, as Baudelaire once called a Paris without friends. Its monumentality, carved out of cold-to-the-touch stone, could overwhelm me, making me feel insignificant by comparison. I sought the company of others, if only to feel less trivial. But sometimes he wasn't there when I showed up. On those occasions, armed with the building's entrance code and becoming a familiar face to the concierge, I wandered over to that part of the building where the grand dame of the Left Bank had once lived, holding court with the greats of her day: Cézanne, Matisse, Picasso, Apollinaire. Her apartment had been in a wing opposite the one where the garret was located, accessible by a private flight of stairs. Once I went right up to the door, made of thick dark wood, and reverently touched it, as I had seen my Irish grandmother touch a station of the cross during one of her pilgrimages to the cathedral in Belfast. Paris was the world city of art. I wanted to be part of it. The desire in me was strong enough that I increased my visits to Tom, listening patiently as he read out loud thinly sketched passages from his work in progress, and peering out the window at the dreamy view. When I had heard enough, I would excuse myself and tee-ter down the hall toward the stinking communal bathroom, shared by other would-be artists upstairs in the Rue de Fleurus building. The bathroom had a missing door. A pile of old newspapers used as wipe lay strewn across the floor. Gertrude Stein and her acolytes had never ascended to this poverty-stricken outpost, I thought. When I returned to the garret, I often found Tom eating hungrily out of a box of granola. About the only meal he could afford.

Danielle, however, lived the bourgeois life on the other side of the Jardin du Luxembourg, on the quiet Rue de Turenne, near the elegant Place des Vosges. The five-room apartment belonged to a well-heeled French roommate, whom she had met at the business school in Fontainebleau. She had gone to the south of France for the season, leaving an empty bed in her wake. Danielle called her BCBG, short for *bon chic, bon genre,* the French equivalent of yuppie. Her third-floor apartment, wrapped around with large win-dows that filled the interior with dazzling light, was newly renovated, with a spacious bathroom sporting a deep bath-tub, a luxury in those days, an en-suite washer and dryer, and a large communal oak dining table where Danielle regularly held court. In Paris, my once plain-Jane friend was queen of her scene.

Like Gertrude before her, Danielle prided herself on "discovering" people. Every Thursday night she opened the doors of her apartment to a throng of strangers who, mostly through word of mouth, came to nibble on her pretzel sticks while rhapsodizing on the fruits of artistic endeavor. I loved this re-creation of a Paris salon and quickly became one of the faithful. Even though I was on a limited budget, I regularly ran out to the corner *épicerie* to buy a bottle of Martini & Rossi, the house aperitif, as well as a carton of Gitanes with which to ply the guests. I helped pour while Danielle, about the only one in the assemblage of imported twenty-somethings with a steady income and a place of her own, sat taller than the rest on a high-backed chair in the middle of her living room. She laid it on thick, I thought as, week after week, I watched her bat her thick lashes at the people sitting cross-legged at her feet. She cooed at them and called them her little birds. Tweet. Tweet. Nobody flinched. They knew about the Rue de Fleurus apartment. She was Gertrude Stein as far as they were concerned, and Danielle, I could see, wanted to believe it. And so these Thursday night parties were a tango of sorts. Danielle gave the would-be artists free booze, and they in turn gave her a sense of superiority that no doubt sustained her through her dull days at work, toiling in obscurity alongside accountants.

Tom was a Thursday-night regular. One night Danielle said that he had a crush on me. I rolled my eyes and made sure to mingle with others in the room. Being social was a new sensation for me. In Toronto I had been withdrawn, avoiding even the pubs and frat parties that were a routine part of campus life. I especially shunned affairs of the heart, thinking they would interfere with my studies and ambition. My mother had taken to calling me a prude. I couldn't argue. I had become a nun to the books. I went to the library, even when I had no homework to do. I was a nerd, and a vegetarian to boot. But in Paris I felt different. I wanted to talk, drink, smoke, party. I wanted to know myself in connection with others. For the most part it was easy to do, because a number of us in Paris that summer, especially those I was meeting at Danielle's, were newly hatched from the cocoon of university life and restless to take on the world. Words erupted from our mouths. It wasn't conversation, exactly. More a series of monologues, with all of us showing off what we knew, what we loved, what turned us on, intellectually speaking. Ideas as sexual foreplay.

HE: What I find interesting about Nathalie Sarraute is that she writes and rewrites what she's written in careful analysis of the very language that she's used.

SHE: I know what you mean. She lets one line drop and hang there on the page for the momentary experience of the imaginary event.

HE: Totally. Sarraute succeeds in isolating fiction like an island in the stream of the everyday.

SHE: Like, this is true to what Barthes says in his *From Work to Text:* the status of writing has to undergo a change that radically alters its function in the past from communication of ideas from author to reader. It's the linguistic unit of the text that matters. The word. You know?

HE: Right on. Hey, can I have your number?

There were no Braques or Matisses among us, no Joyces or Pounds either. But Paris had identified in us a need to bolster our own frailties with magnificence, with brilliance. We were all going to write a book one day, or create a museum-worthy painting. We really believed it. The bravado of our shared youth made us think it infinitely possible. Most of us just didn't know how to go about it yet, and so we continued to pontificate on the meaning of art, as it related to our own as-yet-to-be-formed lives.

But although we were linked by a belief in Paris as the center of the creative universe, the more we sought out each other's company, the more we drifted away from the city, from having a real experience of it. These Thursday-night gatherings were filled with Anglophones, never any French people. Everyone spoke English, myself included. To my shock and dismay, I seemed to have forgotten most of the French I had learned in school. I had dropped it as a course of study after first year university, as it had been hard and I worried the best I would get for all my effort was a B-plus grade. I justified my decision by thinking I would become bilingual after moving back to Paris, where

I assumed I'd speak French with the natives all day along. Wrong. Parisians didn't readily speak with non-Parisians. Besides, I was spending all my time with people from my side of the pond. I spoke English with Danielle, and with Tom, who didn't know one word of French except *bonjour*, and he pronounced it bum-jewer, making it sound like an insult. Occasionally I went with him to one of his hot-spot assignments, one memorable time being the opening of the nightclub Les Bains Douches, where, weirdly, a child performer wore a gold lamé suit and sang "Blue Suede Shoes," but in French. Tom wouldn't have known what the kid was singing if it weren't for the familiar rockabilly beat. But he didn't care. The drinks were on the house, and he ordered one after the other in English. He also spoke English to the taxi driver who drove us back to Rue de Fleurus where, once we were upstairs, he plaintively asked if I would go to bed with him. I said no, the universal word for rejection, and fell asleep on his floor. Later I asked him why he didn't try to speak French, even a little. "Why bother?" he shrugged. "It's an English-speaking world." I saw him, and indeed the rest of us imported Paris-worshippers, as islands of ironic resistance in the French capital—open to the myth of Paris as city of art, but closed to its everyday realities, its otherness.

"Oh, Paris isn't about the French," trilled Danielle, one evening. She wanted to shush my complaint that we were experiencing Paris at a remove, sheltered inside a self-protecting suburb of artistic pretension. "Paris is about living well in any language."

The comment was trite and might have wafted out the open window along with the wispy entrails of our filterless cigarettes. A relative newcomer was among us that Thursday night in Danielle's apartment, and she quickly swatted down the inanity, as if it were a bothersome fly to jerk and sputter on the living room's shag-rug floor.

Lucy was a genuine expat, with more than twenty years' experience living and working in Paris. This made her altogether too jaded for our Thursday gathering. An American who taught American literature to American students at the American academy in Paris, she reminded me of one of those nested wooden dolls that can be reduced to a tiny kernel of the thing itself, except she was bursting at the seams—a big blonde from the Midwest with a too-tight skirt and a mole at the side of her mouth that she had touched up with a pencil to rekindle a fading allure.

"None of you has ventilated an original idea all night," Lucy said, a little too loudly. She threw her head back to exhale the smoke from a stubby Gitane in a long train that stretched to the ceiling. "You," she said, looking at Danielle, "are full of shit."

I regarded her as a woman of unusual dignity.

I went over to her, sprawled in a chair, and asked her about her teaching. The conversation segued into American modern literature, her specialty. She said she loved F. Scott

Fitzgerald because in his writing he identified moral decay as the symptom of a life lived too sweetly on the fruits of material gain. I nodded and, perhaps because I had been drinking myself, blurted that that I would be a writer, too. Might she recommend me for a teaching job at her college to help me stay in Paris? She said she'd do better. She took out a pen from her purse and wrote down the address of Shakespeare and Company, where she said writers could live for free. "The guy who runs it, George Whitman, loves artists, and if you say you're a writer he might let you stay there. Tell him I sent you. And get yourself out of this den of phonies, and fast."

IT WAS MIDAFTERNOON of a sun-dappled day in May when I first arrived at Shakespeare and Company, located directly across from the Notre Dame cathedral, on the banks of the Seine. The bookstore at 37 Rue de la Bûcherie was quiet, despite the steady stream of visitors. Pilgrims in blue jeans shuffled solemnly down the aisles, every step retracing the path of a literary past. I thought, this is where Hemingway pontificated on the black poetry of the bull, where Pound sat hunched on a stool reading and rereading Homer in preparation for his own epic poems, where Fitzgerald and Canada's Morley Callaghan nodded their hellos while reading the papers from back home. I peered into the dark interior and imagined all the artists who had come there, once upon a time, before me.

Except this wasn't where they had really congregated. The place was a facsimile. The original Shakespeare and Company had been located around the corner on the Rue de l'Odéon, serving as bookstore, lending library, and social hub for expat writers between the wars. Its founder and sole proprietor, Sylvia Beach, a transplanted American, made literary history when in 1922 she published Joyce's *Ulysses* through Shakespeare and Company at a time when no one would touch it, thinking its experimental prose style incomprehensible and, in places, pornographic. But not even that claim to fame could save Beach and her bookstore from ruin. In 1941, just before the Nazis imprisoned her for six months in an internment camp at Vittel reserved for American and British citizens, Beach closed down her shop for good, hiding her books in a vacant upstairs apartment at 12 Rue de l'Odéon. Hemingway, it is said, personally "liberated" the bookstore in 1944, but it never reopened. Instead, some twenty years later George Whitman, another American expat who had been in Paris since the end of the Second World War, resurrected it in name only, in 1966 renaming his Le Mistral bookstore after Beach's in tribute to all she had done for modern literature.

No one seemed to mind the lack of authenticity. This shrine of a shrine, housed in a tiny building with small windows and rickety shutters on the Quai de Montebello— what Anaïs Nin once described as a Utrillo house, weak of foundations—is a sanctuary of thought and literary aspirations, a throwback to a lost time. I was reminded of this the minute I met Whitman.

When I arrived at his shop, suitcase in hand, he was on the floor rummaging through cardboard boxes of paperbacks. There was little of the whiff of legend about him. He was thin, gray-haired, his face the color of porridge, his eyes beady, his fingers long and dirty. One of the first things he said to me as I introduced myself was that he was one of the illegitimate children of the great American poet Walt Whitman, hence the name. I tried imagining him as the love child of the great poet.

He then told me that, at nearly seventy years of age, he had recently become a father himself. His daughter was the offspring of his relationship with a woman about forty years his junior. "Met her here," he said, his voice hoarse and crackling. "Like I'm meeting you." He had called the baby Sylvia, after Sylvia Beach, of course.

This was a place dedicated to a memory of Paris as *la bohème,* and accordingly Whitman had two requirements for potential lodgers: you had to be an artist and you had to be living hand to mouth. I was an undergrad, but a published undergrad, my poems in the overwrought style of T.S. Eliot having made it into some of my university's literary publications, so I coolly told him that I was a poet and therefore an artist (check). I assured him I was penniless—it was why I was bed-hopping in Paris, in search of cheap accommodation (check again). I said that come fall, I would be moving permanently to Paris to begin my life as a writer at an English-language magazine. I was certain of it (double check).

"Okay, you can stay. But you have to earn your keep. Everyone here either works in the bookstore or cleans up. You can clean up. Starting tomorrow. I'll show you your bed."

We walked together past a dry wishing well at the center of the store, into which some backpacking tourists were throwing coins. "Live for Humanity" was carved at its base. We continued to the back, past bookshelves yielding to the weight of novels, biographies, cookbooks, art histories, and children's stories crammed together with no apparent system of organization, and soon stumbled upon a hidden circular staircase that Whitman told me led to the communal bedrooms upstairs. It bore another slogan: "Be Not Inhospitable to Strangers Lest They Be Angels in Disguise."

I later learned that Whitman had been the original hippie. After pursuing Latin American studies at Harvard, he had dropped out and gone on a seven-year odyssey through Central America. The hospitality he received as a long-haired stranger among the poor shaped how he in turn treated strangers like me with an unquestioning generosity.

He caught me staring.

"I have always been a communist," he bellowed. "Like Christ. Like my father." I assumed he meant Walt.

"I believe in the religion of art. The rule of freedom. It's why I left America. The puritan work ethic, the need to succeed, to be rich, richer than the next guy. But you don't just earn your living in this life. You live your life."

We climbed the stairs and entered a loftlike space whose walls were lined with books, arranged alphabetically. By day it was the bookstore reading room, a sprawling second floor littered with faded chenille pillows and equally worn divans with colorful crocheted blankets thrown insouciantly on top. At night when the store was closed, these were converted into the beds on which Whitman's acolytes of art would lie in order to be closer to their dreams.

One was already there, sitting cross-legged on his makeshift bed. Whitman grunted an introduction. This was Paulie, from Tallahassee, Florida, my new roommate. Whitman beamed in his direction and called him a surrealist. With his clipped black hair, knee-length shorts, and dazzling orthodontic smile, he did not look like a radical to me. Whitman softened the gruff voice he had used with me. He practically cooed at Paulie to show me his work. He was either right proud of him or, well, quite fond of him, at least. Paulie reached down to pull out a black leather portfolio from underneath the divan. One by one, he laid out a series of rectangular papers displaying intricate drawings of imaginary worlds inhabited by man, beast, and what looked like intergalactic spacecraft. "I am a postcard artist," Paulie said, surprising me with the novelty of his métier. When Whitman left the room, muttering something about the baby needing changing, Paulie patiently handed me miniature after miniature, delighted that I went willingly into his condensed world.

Why small? I wanted to know. Because the world is too big to know it intimately, Paulie responded. All he ever wanted, he said, was intimate knowledge of a thing. "Don't you want that, too?"

Yes, I wanted intimate knowledge. I wanted also knowledge of intimacy. I looked at him, quizzically.

I was to be shacked up with him, it seemed. He on one side of the room, me on the other. There was a softness about him as he bent down to put away his postcards. My mind zigged and zagged like a pinball in an arcade game. Him? Me? I shook my head clear of its annoying clanging. Paulie was talking to me. He was waiting for an answer. "I'm sorry, what did you say?" My face blazed hot with embarrassment.

"I was saying, if you weren't too tired, would you care to go for a walk with me down the Boulevard Saint-Michel. It's my first time in the city, but I've walked a few times, now. It's cool. I'd like to share it with you." I guessed that's what's known as southern charm.

He had a winning smile, despite the braces. "Sure," I said. "I can sleep any time."

And so we strangers, both newly hatched from the cocoon of university life and both around the same age, became instant companions by dint of being in Paris at the same time, and on the same wavelength. We were both drawn to Paris by a quest for immortality through art, an idea that the city, filled with old buildings affixed with plaques commemorating artists who had come there before us, took great pains to highlight. We walked shoulder to shoulder down the tree-lined boulevard, past the Sorbonne and its student bookshops and cafés, aimlessly talking, gamely probing ideas about life and art and existence. Most of this came through a discussion of his work, which I asked him to describe to me. "I use the smallest of brushes," he explained. "I observe the smallest of details." He wasn't alone. He said that there were dozens of artists like him around the world. Paris was just the first stop in a world mini–art tour. Next stop, he told me, was Finland. I was speechless. I had never heard of anything so peculiar. He asked me about myself. I grew self-conscious. If he was an observer of the smallest detail, what would he observe about me? I even became aware of the twists my mouth made when I talked. His sea-green eyes poured right through me, like water.

"Are you an artist, too?"

Artist. I rarely allowed myself the label. But with this earnestly creative soul by my side, I grew emboldened. "Er, yes, well, I write." He encouraged me to tell him more. We were sitting on a bench at the southern tip of the Jardin du Luxembourg. In front of us was the Fontaine de l'Observatoire, a bronze sculpture of four women holding up a globe representing the four continents. Paulie hadn't been to the park before but he knew this flamboyantly public work of art. He remembered that the fountain was in *Gigi*. I had seen the movie but couldn't recall the sculpture. I told him so. But I did know about the artist, Jean-Baptiste Carpeaux, and told Paulie his work also decorated the facade of the Opéra, depicting the spirit of the dance. "How do you know that?" he asked.

I didn't want him to think I was the type of tourist who memorizes guidebooks, but I was. I believed I knew everything there was to know about Paris—from an outsider's perspective at least—by studying it first in books, as I had done on my last trip to Paris. Alone, I had done the walking tours suggested by Fodor's. I had perfected a surface knowledge of the city. Now I wanted intimate knowledge of the thing, as Paulie had so intriguingly put it. I just had to open myself up to the people who inhabited it. "I love dance," I ventured, "and I take care to know as much about it as possible." At that point he reached over and removed a piece of hair that had stuck to my lips. A dog's whistle of sexuality sounded deep inside my brain. I hoped no one else heard it but me. "Thanks," I said. "It's windy in Paris today, isn't it?"

We stopped at the Closerie des Lilas, the celebrated Montparnasse café where Verlaine and Ingres and a whole host of Paris artists used to come, and sat on a pair of cane chairs on the outdoor terrace, shielded by a large awning overhead. I grew worried after a taciturn waiter handed us a menu. A coffee cost almost triple what I was used to paying. Paulie must have sensed that I couldn't afford a place like that. He said, "Please. Order anything you want. My treat. I'm going to have a Coke. With lemon." I said I'd join him, and thank-you.

The sky-high prices underscored that the café was a tourist magnet. I looked around. The terrace was decorated with potted trees, and garlands of vines at the entranceway created a sense of shelter. I noticed others like me, wide-eyed and sitting stiffly, not knowing exactly how to act in a place that was both a clip joint and a slice of Parisian cultural history. When the Cokes arrived, Paulie raised his glass and proposed a toast. "To art," he grinned. "To art," I said. He felt like a kindred spirit. I relaxed and told him about my last four years in Toronto as an under-grad, studying hard, exercising even harder, running eleven miles a day around an indoor track, which he, sucking languidly on a straw, couldn't believe. I explained that I kept myself in a constant state of preparedness in anticipation of the day I would finally leave the ivory tower and go mano-a-mano with the real world lying just beyond the walls of my book-strewn room. But why so punishing? he asked me. I said that I had been a scholar-ship student, expected to maintain an A average if I wanted the university to continue paying for my education. I said that I had been in fear of sliding. I had nothing to fall back on should I fail. And so I had sunk deep inside my imagination, scribbling verse and envisioning lives not yet lived. Lives I believed would unfold in Paris, far from the sterile existence I had chained myself to.

"Oh come on, it couldn't have been that bad," he teased. "Look at you. You know how to be the life of the party."

I soldiered on, wanting to convince him that my life outside of Paris really did suck. I told him about Toronto, describing it as a city of concrete and steel girders, where the streets were denuded of trees and flowers and other symbols of vitality. Toronto, I continued, was where you couldn't drink in a restaurant, not even a glass of wine with dinner, after ten o'clock on a Sunday night. It was where art was seen as frill and where hockey, in the form of a dried-up team optimistically called the Maple Leafs, was what passed as the pinnacle of culture.

"Toronto's a blighted landscape littered with impersonal strip malls, Kentucky Fried Chicken franchises, and desolate pothole-marked parking lots that seem to stretch on forever." He laughed at that. "No, seriously," I said. "It's a soulless place, where I was certain the fire in me would be snuffed out if I stayed."

"But how did you know, then, that you wanted to be a writer?"

I then told him about working nights at the *Varsity*, the student newspaper, where I said my real education had taken place, inside a white, gingerbread-trimmed Victorian house facing the library we called Fort Book. The plaster fell off in chunks from the walls, and the furnishings were threadbare. But that was where I felt the formation of a new identity exploding under the influence of caffeine, trail mix, and aggressive rock and roll piped in from the surly campus radio station located on the floor above the newspaper's offices. For three years, almost all my undergraduate life, I had been dance critic, reporting on performances in and around Toronto and gaining recognition within the community at large as someone who knew what she was talking about. I had loved my studies of Donne, Spenser, Shakespeare, and Blake, I said. But over time the newspaper and its rickety tables topped with Underhill typewriters became all-important to me. Journalism was the glittering light of a key that would open doors to the real world, I said. And my ticket to a job.

"That's why I'm in Paris," I said. "There's an English-language publication here called *Passion,* run by Canadians employing Americans, if you can believe it, all of them expats. I'm going to track them down. I'm going to ask if I can work for them. Beg them, if I have to."

"So, *Passion*'s your destiny, is it?"

I blushed as he paid the bill.

Later that night, back at Shakespeare and Company, we continued our self-excavations. He told me he wanted to be the next Paul Klee. I told him, not imaginatively, that

I wanted to be the next Ernest Hemingway, once a Paris-based reporter for the *Toronto Star*. Settling into our respective places at opposite sides of the upstairs room, our conversation shifted again to art. We spoke of Brancusi and Satie and jazz. Paulie asked me if I thought art needed to be esoteric to be considered worthy of the title. "Is good art the result of impulse and imagination? Or is it a system of codes that only the initiated can or should access?"

I laid my head on my pillow. Hell if I knew. But I decided in that instant to put my money on the inner life. "It usually starts with a dream, doesn't it? A vision of an alternative life?"

I was yawning now, and not just because all this art talk was wearing me down. I had not yet recovered from my transatlantic flight, and desperately needed sleep. I lay on the makeshift bed, and my head brushed up against the wall of books behind me. I turned to read the spines. Author names beginning with B: Beardsley and Beckett and Bemelmans. I didn't know who Bemelmans was, except that it was the name of a Toronto bar where people danced on tables, their panties swinging over their heads. I said the name, "Bemelmans," out loud.

"I know who he is," said Paulie drowsily. "Ludwig Bemelmans is the author of the *Madeline* series of books for girls." Oh yes. The young girl, ward of a convent run by a Miss Clavel, inhabiting Paris and all its wonders.

"Who've you got on your side?" I asked.

"Rilke," he said. And before he could say more, in walked Whitman to bid us goodnight. "It's lights out," he boomed. The literary life as boot camp.

I lay in the darkness thinking of Rilke's *Sonnets to Orpheus,* about how in life you are never supposed to look back, and wondered if it was a mistake coming back to Paris, thinking I could make it there. I also thought of the stranger lying across the room from me. I wondered if something would happen, instead, with him. He was awfully still and quiet. Was I expected to make a move? I lay frozen, contemplating rejection, fearing the noise we might make. I suddenly wanted to write in my journal, to make sense of it all. I felt myself breaking away from my past. I was embracing, at long last, maturity. But when I gently called out Paulie's name, he didn't answer. He was already fast asleep. I was afraid that I would wake him if I turned on the light. And so I started thinking about our day, going over what had been said and unsaid in the dying light of a Paris afternoon.

I had been reckless in telling him about my mother, about how for this trip to Paris she had bought me a new racy red leather jacket plus a pair of black silk pants that she envisioned me wearing on the dance floor of some chic Parisian nightclub. She had never been to Paris but she understood the city as being synonymous with thrill. For the last four years she had been trying to get me out of the study hall and into the discos, where she had been going in search of a good time. She was in her early forties then, in her prime. She regarded Paris as an ally in her goal of turning me into a woman she could relate to—a fun-loving party animal, not the frowning, would-be intellectual darkening her couch with a book in hand each Christmas break.

"You need to get laid," she said concernedly, as if prescribing me an aspirin for a headache. I couldn't believe I had told him that. What had I been thinking? In Toronto I was something of a recluse. In Paris I couldn't keep my mouth shut. I felt ridiculous. And I needed to pee.

Being careful not to disturb Paulie, I tiptoed out of the room we shared, hands feeling my way along the bookcases. I found by touch the railing of the spiral staircase leading down several stories to the only facilities allowed us disciples of art—a Turkish toilet in the basement. I hoped I would make it in time. I made my way down the stairs guided by my sense of smell. What a stench! I couldn't see the footholds that allow you to anchor yourself just inches away from the hole into which goes the day's visits to the café. I must have been off a bit, because I felt the urine spray against my legs as it hit the floor. I quickly leaned forward. And then my head hit a grille on the door. I was looking out at the street. People were walking by, oblivious to my straining. The moon was full, and I could see Notre Dame in the distance. Paulie had got me thinking about point of view. And here I was staring out at a landmark framed by my little window on a toilet door. As a vision of Paris, poetic and noble and true, it was a unique perspective. It quelled my aching brain enough to allow me to fall asleep once I got back upstairs.

"IT'S A BRAND new day! Hip hip hooray!" It was Whitman at the door again. This time he was flicking the lights on and off. What an irritant. It was seven o'clock. I never woke that early, and if I did I was groggy. I was squinting fiercely at the brightness crashing through the room. I saw Paulie and thought to smile, but couldn't; I didn't want him to look at me. I didn't want to look at him. We had talked so much the day before. Thinking I had perhaps overdone it, shared too much of myself, I could barely pronounce a proper good morning.

But these two Americans could. They were perfectly polite with each other. As an added courtesy, Whitman had even brought Paulie a bowl of steaming café au lait and two buttery croissants, kept warm beneath a folded napkin. Room service. There was nothing for me. I assumed it was because Paulie had already been there a week, so Whitman had gotten to know him. I saw how he looked at Paulie, his gaze sticky as caramel. I glanced in Paulie's direction. I thought he must be ignoring me. He sat on the edge of the divan with head lowered, quietly eating a croissant that he tore into bird-sized pieces, minuscule as his art. As I hastily grabbed some clothes to change into beneath my sheets, I thought that perhaps Paulie was again being gentlemanly.

By not looking at me, he was allowing me some privacy. That must be it.

"I'll, um, see you later, okay?" I called out as I grabbed my knapsack and headed for the stairs. He raised a mute hand and waved.

Out on the corner, at a local café, I purchased my own café crème and croissant for a few francs. I stared blankly out the window at the passersby. My first morning of the artist's life, and already I felt lonely.

I decided to go to the Place de l'Opéra, to look again at the dancing sculptures I had described to Paulie from memory the day before. I ran down the stairs leading to the metro, past a classical violinist and a mime artist with painted tears falling from his eyes. I hurriedly took in the cardboard sign held in the dirty hands of a shivering beggar: *J'ai faim*, I am hungry. The words were written in that distinctly French, flowery style. God, I thought, even the downtrodden in Paris have savoir faire. I clinked a coin into his cup and continued forward, past large colored posters of pouting women in their push-up bras and other smaller-scale announcements advertising an abundance of music concerts unfolding that week at city churches. Sex and art. I was back in Paris all right, where the sacred and the profane commingled.

My brain switched channels. Standing on the platform in a crush of patrons, I imagined my red leather jacket to be a cape daring bulls to charge my way, penetrate my armor.

I had danger on my mind and my mother, in large part, to thank for it. For the last four years I had been seeing in black and white, but suddenly I was seeing in Technicolor. I marvelled at how a simple change of environment had such a galvanizing effect on my being. I had made the right choice. Yes. This was really going to work out. I inhaled deeply, sucking in the pungent odor of the Paris metro, a noxious brew of burnt rubber, unwashed hair, and wool jackets perpetually dampened by rain. The aroma of the masses. I inhaled it as if it were the sweetest incense, vitalized by thoughts of revolution—my own personal one, that is.

And then, whoosh. In a Proustian moment, I travelled back in time, to four years earlier during my first trip to Paris. I remembered the short, swarthy man sitting opposite me on an eastbound train who had been hissing at me to get my attention. I had made the mistake of glancing up at him, and this had given him encouragement. He was on me like a fly on a raw piece of meat. I kept my nose primly in a book, thinking that would make him go away, lose interest. But he was rudely insistent. He pestered me to know where I was from. "Canada," I had huffily answered, thinking that would squash him. But my answer had unexpectedly made him laugh out loud. He turned in his seat and to the rest of the passengers riding the second-class car loudly proclaimed me "Miss Canada Dry." They all laughed. A joke. That's how Paris had seen me, then. Mortified, at the next station I had exited the train, pretending it was my stop. I walked determinedly up the stairs, believing I was being watched.

I snapped back to the present. How self-conscious I used to be. I smiled bitterly at the memory. I was older now, wiser—or so I hoped, four years later. Paris was still pretty much the same. There, right in front of me on the platform, was another man, quietly looking. But I had changed. I wouldn't give him a chance to say anything, not one word. I haughtily looked away, feigning self-confidence. I would never be Miss Canada Dry again.

Returning a few hours later to Shakespeare and Company, I saw Whitman sitting at a table at the front of the shop, tinkling the change in the cash register. When he saw me staring, he lurched to his feet and came close to me. I saw that the stubble on his chin had some red in it, vestige of a more virile past. He was breathing on me—the rotten smell of hash oil.

"Earn your keep, remember?"

I stiffened as he grabbed my arm. What did he mean? He shoved a stick into my hand. "Give her a steady whack until it comes off."

"Pardon?"

"The carpets, you silly she-person. The carpets!" He pointed a gnarled finger to what was underfoot.

Oh. I was to beat the carpets. Okay. Whew. I got on my hands and knees to roll one up. Paulie appeared and bent down beside me. "Hi," he said softly. "Let me help you."

Holding one end of the carpet, he walked past Whitman without a glance. I meekly followed him outdoors, hoisting my end. I had to blink several times to get used to the sharp slant of midmorning sun that was bouncing off the Seine in diamond patterns of light. It was blinding, and I had difficulty flinging the carpet onto the railing of the balustrade flanking the river.

"One, two, three—ho!" Paulie was now guiding my efforts. How nice, I thought, for him to help me. Surely Whitman must have given him other chores to do to earn his keep. I asked him. "Oh, I mostly sit in the bookstore, minding the cash. But really I just read," he said. "Don't mind George. He's not the terror he makes out to be. He's really too soft. That's why he talks that way. He's trying not to show his feminine side."

I wondered if Paulie was joking. He had a sly grin on his face. But now the hard work began. With each thwack of the stick, thick clouds of dust rose into the air, choking us both into silence. This was the dirt the Shakespeare and Company acolytes had left behind after wiping their sandals at the door. I was being covered in gossamer layers of their skin cells, their sweat, their strands of hair dropped at the threshold. I didn't know if this was an anointing or a poisoning of my senses. Certainly the artistic life, as practiced in this corner of Paris, wasn't the glamorous adventure I had imagined back in Canada. I would always have hard work, I realized. I would always have days of feeling underslept and underfed. But did I also have to stoop to cleaning other people's crap?

"I think this carpet is as clean as it will get," I said to Paulie. He helped me carry the beast back into the bookstore. We couldn't go back up to the room we shared; it was now open to the public. There they were again, the pilgrims, reverently mooning about the place as if it were a church.

Paulie suggested we go outside to the pretty little park next door. It was a boxy slice of green, accessed through a gate you had to open and shut with a clang of its bolt. A gurgling fountain lay at its center. Close by was the Romanesque Saint-Julien-le-Pauvre, one of the oldest churches in Paris, where a noonday concert of chamber music was underway. I could hear the complex syncopations of Bach rising on the breeze. Paulie lay on the grass. He motioned for me to do so as well. "What do you see?" He was staring up at the sky, at the meringues of clouds silently floating by. I hadn't played this game since childhood. I could see a woman with a long crooked nose. Paulie saw a ship at sea. "It is crashing into a long slow wave. A sailor has already gone overboard. See him? That speck over there?" He was pointing upward at a bit of heavenly fluff.

I couldn't see what he was talking about. "Where?"

He leaned over and gently pulled my face toward his. I thought he would kiss me, then. My body stiffened with anticipation. But instead he kept turning me until he felt that my eyes were finally in the right place. "Now do you see?" I saw it now, a galleon and a typhoon and, if I gave into the illusion a little bit more, yes, a sailor struggling in the waves. Trying not to drown. The sun felt hot on my body. I lay there under that quiet storm erupting overhead and thought that I had found a perfect kind of peace.

Later that night, after he had crawled into his bed and I into mine, and hours after Whitman had charged us with the killing of the lights, Paulie whispered my name, and I went over to him. There was no talking this time. His kisses were like microscopes, unmasking fear and magnifying desire. A dot connecting with another dot in the universe's blinding swirl. I let myself go.

HE WAS GONE by the time I woke the next day on my side of the room, having moved back to my bed in the pitch of night. Whitman observed the bewildered expression on my face. He had brought me a coffee this time and, as he handed it to me, he explained that Paulie had left before sunrise, taking a taxi to the airport. I imagined him inside the airplane, next stop Finland, hurtling through space in search of other intimate worlds to explore and conquer, merging with the clouds that had so fired his imagination the day before. I would never see or hear from him again. Not even a postcard.

I desultorily dressed myself and my bed, returning the pillows and the quilted cover heaped on the floor. I headed out the door to walk through the Latin Quarter, commune with my thoughts. It was still early. The market on nearby Rue de Buci was preparing to open. Shellfish were lined in neat armylike rows on beds of crushed ice and halved lemons. I could smell the brine on the morning air. A street cleaner was pouring water over the ancient cobblestones and, with a witch's broom made of gangly red-brown branches, was sweeping the previous night's debris into the gutter.

I headed for the Jardin du Luxembourg, inhaling the first vapors of that day's exhaust. I was wearing my red leather jacket. It flew open in the wind as I walked, everyone else around me prim and busily heading to their office jobs, a hive of industry buzzing around me. For once, I was standing on the outside of all that demanding assiduousness. I had had sex with a stranger. I felt decadent, like I had suddenly joined the ranks of the demimonde. Fatigue overwhelmed me, as did a feeling of ineptitude. I wondered why my mother had wanted me to gain experience this way. I didn't feel more grown up. I felt disenchanted— or was that the point? When I called *Passion* later that day, the person on the other end of the phone told me they weren't hiring. They were closing down. The dream, she said, was over.

THE NEXT DAY I waited in line for over an hour in a telecommunications office to call my mother, collect. I was running out of the money I had won in my final weeks as an undergrad. I needed her to wire more. It was one of those crackling overseas calls, and I had to shout out loud that I wasn't coming back home, that I was going to stay and be a writer in Paris, really give it a go. She shouted back that I was making the mistake of my life. She appealed to me to listen to reason. While I had been away, I had been accepted into graduate school, again on scholarship. She had taken the liberty of sending in my acceptance.

"You need to get that higher degree," she said. "To show you're a cut above, which you are. We both are."

I argued some more, the booth feeling hot and confining. I felt I had to hang on to the dream. I told her how beautiful the city was. How it was changing me. "I'm becoming a woman here," I said, thinking that might make her proud.

But she hammered away at her point. "You haven't a job and you haven't any money, and let me tell you something about that fact of life, you never seem to give it much thought, lost in your world of books and make-believe. When you don't have money, life is miserable. Even Paris can feel like a trap if you can't eat or go to all the nice places you are telling me about. Believe you me, four walls in Paris will look as depressing as four walls in Toronto if you can't go out and enjoy yourself."

I knew she was right. I recalled the stench of the Turkish toilet, the rumors of bedbugs. I didn't come to Paris for a life of squalor. I wanted the world of ideal beauty that

Paris still represented to me. In that phone booth I suddenly did an about-face. I shouted at my mother suddenly that she had convinced me. I had a return ticket, after all. "But just for a year, to finish the master's. And then I'm coming back," I wailed.

"Of course you will," my mother clucked. "Because Paris will always be there, waiting for you."

Whitman said something of the same when I went to bid him adieu. "There'll always be a bed here for you," he smiled. "Come back next year, when Sylvia will be quoting her granddaddy Walt, "I sing the body electric." I said he could count on it. The old man looked at me searchingly, as if trying to make sure I meant it. Reaching out to me with a gnarled hand, he touched my cheek, softly patting it in good-bye. I pushed past the day's stream of pilgrims waiting their turn to come in and browse. To feel, for even just a fleeting moment in time, the magic. I knew not to look back.

THREE

Material Girl

· 1986 ·

THE NEWSROOM AT *The Globe and Mail* thrummed with noise. Telephones rang. Radios blared. Men—and there were mostly men working there in those days—cursed and slammed desk drawers sheltering bottles of rye. I didn't have a desk. When I first arrived at Canada's national newspaper, immediately upon graduating with a master's degree in English—my dream of becoming a journalist unfolding in Toronto, and not in Paris as I had expected—the editor in charge just told me to find a desk not in use. "Every man for himself," he grumbled, before yelling at someone to bring him the day's proofs. I roamed the newsroom in search of a place where I could type out, one finger at a time, my stories. I passed by the darkroom, where the bastion of male photographers had postered the walls with bare-breasted pinups, and also the windowless alcove where teletype machines rattled as they spewed endless streams of wire copy onto a grime-thick floor.

I came upon the film critic, perched over a keyboard at one of the few desks supporting a word processor. Absorbed in thought, he bit down on a cigarette, as he raucously typed, and was seemingly oblivious to the long tail of ash that fell with a hush on the keys as he pounded out his review. He hit the send button, releasing his words to an editor, and abandoned the desk. I pounced. The chair was still warm. I blew hard over the letters to make them less dirty. Just then a mouse, black as print, scurried over the keys. It had been nesting in one of the drawers in a bed of chewed-up clippings. A veteran crime reporter sitting next to me laughed when I shrieked. Leaning far back in his chair, he stretched his legs out in front of him, using my new-found desk as a footrest and issuing a challenge. "Do you mind?" I said, eyeing his dirty soles with a look of prissy disdain. It was all I could think to say. He pulled away, leaving me alone. I had claimed my turf. Every day afterward, whenever I came into the newsroom, as soon as he saw me he dragged his feet off the desk that he was reserving for me in his menacing way, soon enabling me to be as productive as the best of them.

It was 1985. The world was climbing out of a recession. Confidence had muscled itself back in, and it wasn't long before I felt caught up in the fast-forward motion of the times. As soon as I started at the paper, in the first days of January, I was busy. I covered dance, my specialty, as well as pop music, theater, and fashion. I also had my own daily entertainment column, launched that fall during the Toronto International Film Festival, highlighting my new life in the orbit of celebrity. I was hobnobbing with the playwright Arthur Miller and the actor Raymond Burr, the crooner Tony Bennett and the American choreographer Paul Taylor, the filmmakers Alan Rudolph and Brian De Palma, and the Russian prima ballerina, Natalia Makarova, a dance-world superstar, as well as the pop diva Chaka Khan. I went day and night to screenings and rock concerts and parties. By the end of the year I had churned out close to two hundred bylined articles, an impressive number considering the paper only came out six times a week. My life seemed to have taken on a momentum all its own. I was no longer indigent, no longer a wallflower. I was salaried, with a closet full of new, expensive clothes. I also had a growing reputation as an upstart. I wrote from the hip, even trashing a recent production of *The Nutcracker*. Soon angry letters to the editor poured in from the barefoot team, the modern dance brigade. They were upset about what they called my callowness, saying I was too young to have so much power. They said my style of criticism, which I thought fearless, but they called reckless, was costing them their Canada Council grants. They demanded I be reassigned, or else, said one independent choreographer leading the charge in an interview on CBC radio, I would be physically removed from the theater if I dared show up to cover any more of their shows. The newsroom applauded. "Way to go, kid," said an especially crotchety newsman, patting me on the back. "You've earned your stripes."

So it was the right career path. I loved the pace. I fed on the natural-born aggression of the newsroom. I fit in, despite a proclivity for designer dresses. It should have made me deliriously content, wanting for nothing. But when there wasn't a deadline or a show to cover, no Alice Cooper phoning me long-distance from a tour stop in Japan, I panicked. I found that I couldn't bear being alone in my own apartment. I didn't know what to do with myself, which, in large part, was why I worked so hard—to keep myself distracted from the feeling that deep down, I felt dissatisfied. Lost. Devoid of meaning. Sure there were suitors, more than there had ever been. I was young and spirited. I had, as my editor told me, great gams. Some of the guys at work had a bet going as to who would be the first one to ask me out. To all appearances I was suddenly popular. But I kept thinking there was something missing.

I might not have been able to put my finger on it, if it weren't for the letters. They were wispy things, written in a faint, slanted hand on thin blue paper, the envelope stamped "airmail." Little by little they had started arriving about a year earlier, when I was finishing off the last of my university courses. They were from Stefano, someone with whom I had indulged a brief fling, only a few weeks long, during a summer undergraduate course in Siena. He was originally from Switzerland and spoke German as well as Italian, languages I had no knowledge of. His English was weak, and so we hardly ever spoke at all, communicating mostly just with our bodies in the darkness of a threadbare apartment overlooking the lush Tuscan hills. I had liked the foreignness of him, as well as his physical beauty. He was muscular, with golden wavy hair and lips as roundly sculpted as those of Michelangelo's *David*. But I quickly grew bored. He might have been sex on two legs (he told me that in Italy he sometimes worked as a gigolo, servicing mostly older American women whom he, startling me with a sudden command of the English language, described as succubi), but I churlishly wanted more in the way of intellectual stimulation. I wanted to share ideas. When I was about to return to Toronto, he had asked for my address, and I gave it to him, not really thinking he would write. But he did.

The letters came in a trickle at first. Then, after I once wrote back, mostly from guilt, they arrived in a torrent of love-soaked words. He declared eternal devotion. He called me his angel on earth. He said he was waiting for me. I thought that silly. I had no intention of running back to him. But as my life as hard-nosed journalist began to rapidly unfold, taking me farther away from my dream of becoming an artist, I began to look forward to those passionate missives from abroad, even taking them with me into the newsroom where I would read them quietly, in the midst of all that tumult, and think of the path not taken. My life had become complicated, weighed down by consumer products and pursuits. His world, by contrast, had stayed simple, true to some eternal truth. He signed his letters "love" and, on the back, often sketched some ancient Italian vista—ruins amid the cypress trees. Meanwhile my editor shouted for his copy. The phone wouldn't stop ringing. Was this it? The rest of my life? I refolded the letter, delicate as tissue, and put it back into my purse. *Love.* It wasn't a word spoken of much at the newspaper. *Love.* It made me yearn for something more.

I knew I couldn't tell anyone about Stefano, my phantom lover. My friends would just laugh. Me. The academic turned careerist. Willing to throw it all away, and for a stud. But secrets aren't secrets if you can't share them with at least one person. I chose my pair of ears, perhaps not so wisely. I told my mother. Her response wasn't at all what I expected. She urged me to go after him. She told me I was crazy not to. Those letters are so beautiful, she said. A gift. She was smitten by the Tarzan-like idea of him, the pretty sketches. Said I was lucky, that I ought to cherish what he was offering me, because it was rare in this cut-throat world of ours. "Wish it were me," she said. At that time, there were no romantics in her corner. She was back to having affairs with married men. "Safer," she told me. "No strings attached." She persuaded me to give my long-distance affair a chance, in order to avoid becoming like her. January 1986 marked my first-year anniversary at the paper. It was also the month I turned twenty-six. For my birthday my mother squeezed a little money into my hand for a ticket to see him. "Go," she urged me. "Find love."

I sent a telegram, telling Stefano I would be coming to see him. He had moved back to Zurich and, in a telegram back, suggested I meet him there, in his hometown. He had a real job now, working in a home for the mentally challenged, feeding them, dressing them, wheeling them through gardens. A life of charity. But I didn't want to know any more about that. This was a quest for romance. I didn't want to go to a city that seemed unsympathetic to that spirit. I wanted to go to Paris, the city that to me most symbolized beauty and desire.

I still imagined I would one day live there. I hadn't given up on that dream, despite landing a full-time job in Toronto right out of university. *The Globe and Mail* didn't have a Paris office. But I imagined that it might. With the economy continuing to improve, the paper was in the midst of opening up a number of new foreign bureaus. I had let my editor know of my interest in Paris. He in turn told me about the Journalistes en Europe fellowship program, enabling foreign journalists to study mass communication at the Sorbonne for a year. This seemed custom-made for me. I had missed the deadline to apply for the 1986 program, but was keen on applying for the following year. I wanted to know if it would be possible to live in Europe with Stefano. Was he really my destiny? Was Paris? In my mind I had started to conflate the two. Both represented the same thing. They were objects of desire, utopian ideals. When I thought of Stefano, he was no longer the person who incessantly played on his portable tape recorder "Video Killed the Radio Star" by British synthpop group The Buggles. I had hated that song. It was what had convinced me that we were never to be. We didn't like the same kind of music. Three years later I had switched mental gears. Or maybe I wasn't thinking at all, not rationally anyway. Ignoring my initial instincts, I willed myself to follow a fiction, an idea of Stefano as the personification of love. I had just been too intellectual the last time, I told myself. I had been too self-conscious. I hadn't opened my heart.

Stefano had said that all he could spare would be a weekend in Paris. I was to meet him on a Friday afternoon, when he would take the train in from Zurich. I figured that would be about the right amount of time to sort out the rest of my life. I bought an air ticket for a five-day stay. I would get there two days early, and until Stefano arrived and I relocated to a hotel, I would stay with a friend who had moved to Paris to work in the fashion industry. I was scheduled to arrive mid-February, around the time the ready-to-wear collections were being staged in Paris at the Louvre. My friend Tova worked at that time for a big-name designer and said she'd be swamped and wouldn't have much time to socialize. But she offered me the keys to her place, where she said she didn't have a bed, just a futon on the floor. "But it's very central," she emphasized. "And you'll have the place pretty much to yourself."

We had discussed these arrangements over the telephone, a straightforward 20th-century thing to do. After I hung up, I realized that I had never picked up the phone to dial Stefano. Partly it was because of the language barrier. But after I thought of it, I supposed that I had preferred him at a remove, a long-distance letter that I waited for, an emotional experience crystallized in images and feathery words. On the plane ride over I worried that I might not be able to tolerate the reality of him any more than I had the first time, almost three years earlier. I thought of the me then, and the me who had boarded the plane that evening with a new set of black Mandarina Duck rubberized luggage bought expressly for the trip. I also had a Walkman and a separate carrying case for all my makeup. When Stefano had seen me last, I didn't wear makeup. I didn't even pluck my brows. I had had just two changes of clothes. I had worn flat-soled sandals that made him call me his little Roman gladiator. I was bookish, idealistic, a student with no obligations except to the books. Life had changed since then. I now had credit cards and debt. I had grown used to eating out in expensive restaurants, going to premieres, mingling with stars, driving in white stretch limousines, flying to New York just to catch a show. I no longer wrote poetry. I hadn't read a novel in years. Who had time? I looked out the window at the night sky and saw a starless black hole. I felt a twinge of panic. I hoped against hope that I was doing the right thing.

WHEN I ARRIVED in Paris, I took a taxi from the airport to Tova's. It was early morning. The sky was low and gray, the dead of winter. There was no snow on the ground, but the streets of Paris looked pale and petrified, as if frozen in time. There was no human life, save for the shadowy figures of uniformed men hauling brooms and dustpans with which to clean away the frost that clung like spiderwebs to the columns and arches of the still-sleeping city. Devoid of people, Paris was a solid mass of stone and glass and shuttered windows. It slipped by me silently behind the glass of my cab window. The driver expertly maneuvered the twisting corridors around the *Arc de Triomphe,* still as an ice sculpture. I took in the chiselled detail on its massive walls—winged angels blowing trumpets, naked boy soldiers clutching their swords. We continued down the Champs-Élysées, sleek and elegant, a street paved with money. We passed the Jardin des Tuileries, where the trees and chairs that surrounded the ice-covered fountains sat dormant, waiting for the sun to come back out. We turned onto a bridge spanning the turbulent Seine. Our destination was the Marais, where Tova lived on the tiny Rue du Bourg Tibourg, near the Hôtel de Ville. It was a residential area, intimate, familiar, with *boulangeries* already drawing people into their brightly lit interiors to buy freshly baked baguettes and croissants still warm from the oven. My taxi pulled up at the corner, in front of a café where the windows were thick with steam rising from the tidy lineup of bodies inside.

I was hoping that Tova would have coffee ready for me when I buzzed her apartment from a downstairs intercom. The entrance door clicked, and I entered her pristine white building, hauling my bags up two flights of immaculate stairs. I could feel my fatigue. I hadn't slept a wink on the plane ride over, too consumed by nerves. My stomach was still in knots when I knocked on her door. I felt weak and winded. My head whirled like a top. Tova pushed open the door and, flashing me a big toothy smile, pulled me quickly into a friendly hug. In that instant I felt better, just knowing I was with someone I knew. She rushed me in, marvelling at the amount of luggage. "There's not really room for the three of us," she said with a laugh that made her head of light brown curls slither and shake around her narrow shoulders. I looked around the apartment. It was small and spare, the only furniture a navy-blue divan pushed up against a wall. A rolled-up futon was in a corner of the room, heaped with blankets. I assumed this was my bed, for a couple of nights, anyway. The air felt clammy and cool. There was no coffee. No warmth apart from Tova's fleeting embrace.

When she had held me close, I had felt the bones protruding through her sweater, which, along with her leggings and ankle boots, was black. A uniform of chic. Her skin seemed almost translucent, and her hands were ice cold to the touch. I figured she was back to her old habit of purging after she ate. She had done that when we lived together in residence at university, and I never understood it. She was beautiful, with sky-blue eyes and dark lashes, a gently sloped nose and a mouth shaped like a rose. She loved beauty, wearable beauty, and ever since I had known her, she had wanted to work in fashion. She had first moved to the city over five years previously to get away from her upper-middle-class parents. It had been her dream to work in fashion, and now she worked for a big-name designer. I had assumed she'd be happy. But her thinness made me wonder. She caught me staring. "I can't be late," she said, quickly wrapping her body in a high-collar coat that she buttoned up to the throat. "Just unroll the futon and get some sleep. I won't be back until very late, anyway. There's a restaurant across the street in case you get hungry."

She laid a key down on a counter inside her minuscule kitchen, alongside some Paris guidebooks. "I got them for you," Tova continued, "to help you find a hotel. When's he coming again?"

"On Friday," I said. "In two days. Will I get to spend some time with you before then?" I asked.

She explained that packs of American buyers were arriving over the next few days to see her boss's new collection at his Left Bank atelier. She had to buy fruit and flowers and champagne, as well as walk the dog. She had so much to do. She looked at the watch that encircled her slender wrist. "Oh, and right now I have to run and get Jean-Claude's dry cleaning on my way into work." She snapped her handbag shut. She threw a scarf around her neck. She reached out to air-kiss me on both sides of the face. I felt buffeted by her swirling storm of perfumed chaos. "And don't wait up for me tonight," she said as she was about to rush out the door. "If he needs me, I might even have to sleep at the atelier tonight. It's a very busy time. You know what it's like."

And then she was gone. The room was suddenly deathly quiet. I didn't know what to do with myself. Her studio apartment faced directly onto the street. I peeled back the gauzy white curtains and for a few minutes watched people scurrying by on the cobblestones below. Paris was fully awake. I saw the restaurant that Tova had mentioned. It was right there, on the corner of Rue du Bourg Tibourg and Rue de la Verrerie, which was handy, I thought after opening her miniature refrigerator and finding only a half-full bottle of Evian and a bunch of wilted celery. I had some packets of peanuts saved from the flight and I put a handful into my mouth. I took one of the guidebooks and started to leaf through it. I was in Paris on a mission, but I was also on a holiday. I didn't have to get busy if I didn't want to. I could take the morning off. I unzipped my carry-on, and pulled out a nightgown. My eyes felt heavy. I unrolled the futon, laying it under the window as Tova had directed, and then fell asleep clutching my blankets.

It was late afternoon when I awoke. I was starving. I dressed quickly and went outside. I thought to walk a bit, get my bearings. I hadn't been to Paris in winter before. The air was damp and biting, and the cold pierced through my woolen Canadian coat and into my bones. I was shivering within minutes. To hell with exteriors, I thought; I needed to get myself inside someplace warm, and fast. I quickly backtracked, entering the restaurant across the street from Tova's apartment building. The interior was instantly comforting. The restaurant had upholstered booths, and a brass railing ran around the mirrored bar, which gleamed in the late-afternoon sun slanting through the front window. I could hear the sound of exploding steam for the making of café au lait. I could smell the hazy aroma of onion soup and decided to order some. I polished one off and, on my waiter's recommendation, also devoured a tarte Tatin, a warmed upside-down apple cake that was a discovery for me. Over the next couple of days I would return repeatedly for more tarte Tatin, more hot cups of coffee, feeling myself get fat. But I didn't care. Eating seemed the only way to keep the unexpected iciness of Paris at bay.

I headed back outside armed with a winter-proof plan. I would go and see a few hotels that I could duck into for temporary refuge against the cold while also determining their suitability for an amorous encounter. I had one of Tova's guidebooks with me and zeroed in on places where the word "romantic" figured large in the descriptive paragraph below the picture. One such hotel was in Saint-Germain and was called Relais Christine, after the street it was located on. I read that it had been home to Alice B. Toklas after Gertrude Stein had died. I thought that a wonderful coincidence considering my last time in Paris. And so I happily set off in search of it. It was just on the other side of the river, not far away, but it wasn't long before pushing through gale winds felt like a chore.

The wind slapped my face and ravaged my hair. The cold pinched my nose, making it hurt, and stung my eyes, making them swell with false tears that rolled down my cheeks. I felt the cold here, perhaps because the air was so damp. The dampness penetrated through all the layers of my clothing, straight to my bones. And there was no central heating anywhere, so I never felt warm. Compounding the situation for a lily-livered North American like myself was the fact that the city is made of cold-to-the-touch stone. I stood on the Pont Neuf and shivered as I peered into the fog threatening to obscure the massive figure of Notre Dame before me. I wondered if it was the jet lag, because I felt weary standing there, jostled by passersby. I also felt curiously bereft of the wonder that Paris had inspired in me on previous trips. I had wandered past Shakespeare and Company but had felt no need to go in. I had seen a door knocker shaped like a Medusa head on the Rue des Saints-Pères and, where once such a thing might have compelled me to think of Paris as a city whose beauty lay in the details, this time I saw kitsch. The weather certainly wasn't conducive to dreaming, especially not out on the slippery sidewalks. I gripped the bridge railing and looked down into the churning waters. If I was looking for my reflection, it wasn't a good omen. The river was muddy. I felt lost to the person I once was. I pulled up the collar of my coat and trudged on.

The hotel, when I found it on Rue Christine, looked instantly inviting. It had large exterior walls with a black wrought-iron gate that you had to push open to enter a secluded courtyard. The front doors were made of glass, and I could see the warmth of the orange-and-red decor inside. It was a four-star hotel and would no doubt provide the kind of elevated service I had lately gotten used to on my expense-account jaunts for the newspaper. But I was shocked when I heard the price, more than $200 a night. This was a level of Paris luxury I could ill afford. I bowed out politely, asking myself what was I thinking? In Toronto

I was already living beyond my means, as evidenced by the bills I could barely pay each month. Such was the high life I had recently, wholeheartedly embraced. There was a new 1980s standard of living that I unquestioningly subscribed to. It was a time when the clubs were full, when the fashions clung like plastic wrap, and when the new perfumes were called Obsession and Poison. Everyone seemed to be on the make. Doing blow. Playing the stock market. Sleeping around. I had wanted to be an exception, but as I continued wandering the tiny streets of Saint-Germain, venturing into more select hotels, the Lenox and the Angleterre, each beyond reach, I realized that I had become bewitched by extravagance. I needed to rethink my strategy.

I pulled into a tiny bistro on the Rue du Bac where there were just a few tables and a red-faced proprietress behind the bar, vigorously wiping her counter clean. I ordered a *tisane*, an herbal tea, wrapping my hands around the ceramic cup to keep warm. I opened up the guidebook, this time concentrating on price point, not ambience. I saw something cheap, very cheap, called the Hôtel Henri IV. It was located on the Place Dauphine, described as a park-like oasis near the Pont Neuf, which I had just wandered away from. I wondered how I had missed it. Or why I had never even heard of it before, despite two previous trips spent combing the hideaways of Paris.

I retraced my steps within minutes and found the triangular-shaped enclave located just beyond the river's edge. It was lined with tall skinny buildings with shutters that looked in danger of falling off. The six-storey hotel at the center was the worst-looking one on the square. The plaque on the outside wall said that the rickety old building once housed the printing press belonging to Henri IV, former king of France, meaning it was more than three hundred years old. And it looked it. The outside plaster was falling off in chunks, and inside the floors were raised and crooked, a veritable house of cards. The lobby was so dark it took a while for my eyes to be able to take in the full scope of the hotel's seediness. The chairs were worn-out, and the wallpaper was peeling. And yet I was seized by a feeling of nostalgia. The Hôtel Henri IV was precisely the kind of place I would have relished if I had discovered it just a few years earlier, during my naive student days. It reeked of Old World authenticity. Dingy. Dilapidated. With communal toilets. And a historic pedigree, to boot. I walked up four flights with the surly hotel owner, stubbornly fixated on the romance of the place. I saw that the upstairs rooms were bright and airy, despite being frayed around the edges. In that moment, feeling out of synch both with myself and Paris, I believed it was exactly what I had been looking for. I hastily booked a double room, putting down a deposit. I convinced myself that Stefano would like it, as well. It seemed custom-made to the pursuit of a lost dream.

My immediate task accomplished, I had nothing else to do. The Paris night stretched before me, taunting me with boredom. I needed to keep moving, to keep from feeling depressed, but the cold was getting to me again. I needed a distraction, and I spied it in La Samaritaine, Paris's largest department store, situated on the opposite side of the Seine. A mixture of art deco and art nouveau architectural styles, it was a large boxy building of several floors, constructed from large expanses of glass held together by a corseting of steel rods. Its domed roof twinkled in the encroaching darkness, beckoning me back across the river and onto the Rue de la Monnaie, the street of money. I entered through a revolving door and found myself in the cosmetics department. Color. Light. Scent. It was as if I had immediately arrived at a carnival. Every bottle, every iridescent jar boasting some magical elixir, called to me. I felt myself calming down a bit, my inner self cajoled into thinking I was in safe territory, a familiar place, having in Toronto become something of a cosmetics junkie. But my composure cracked at the Orlane counter when I looked in the mirror and saw my own eyes looking back at me with sadness, as if part of me knew that in Paris I was courting a masquerade.

"*Bonjour Madame.*"

"*Er, bonjour.*"

"*Cherchez-vous quelque chose en particulier? Puis-je vous aider?*"

I felt flustered. I had been alone with my thoughts, not thinking in French. What was the word for just looking?

"*Um, je ... je ... ne cherche rien. Je veux juste regarder.*"

I sounded like an imbecile. In the mirror I could see that I had started to blush. Parisian saleswomen are an intimidating lot. I suddenly felt awfully hot inside my winter coat.

"You have a very dehydrated *peau*," pronounced my red-haired interlocutor, sliding into a slippery grasp of English. She had reached over to stroke my face with one of her manicured nails. A frown creased her perfectly plucked eyebrows as she intently studied my face. She smelled like gardenias. I was overcome by her scent when she gently put her hand under my chin and pulled me expertly forward, catching me unawares in her snare. At the cosmetics counter in Paris I had met a Siren.

"The pores, they are big, and the *épiderme* is, how would you say? Scaly."

I jumped a little in that skin she was now describing as if it were a snake's.

"*S'il vous plaît,* to sit down."

She motioned to a tall white chair that was beside an enormous palette of lipstick shades displayed as greasy dots of eye-popping color. There were also small pots of red and pink blush, as well as a deployment of sharply pointed eyeliner pencils in black, brown, gray, turquoise, emerald, and sapphire blue. I was transfixed as if by a rainbow. I wondered if she would use these pigments on me, turn me into one of the peacocks that decorated an overhead mural.

She caught me looking at her tray of goodies.

"First we need to disencrust ze surface." I knew what she meant, but this direct translation from the French made me feel that my face was a crater moon, full of volcanic ash. If I had been feeling bad that day, I suddenly felt worse. But she already had me bibbed, with a clip in my hair to hold back my unruly bangs. I couldn't flee. She stood behind me and lowered my head backwards. I closed my eyes as she began massaging me with oil that she hurriedly wiped off with a tissue. That she followed with a cream that felt as if it had particles of sand in it. The exfoliant. "Please to relax," she intoned. Her voice was low and seductive. "With this *crème*," she continued, "I will *protège* your juvenility." How had she known? I would buy anything now, as long as she made me feel eternally youthful. I thought to myself how good it was that she had found me.

Her hands moved rapidly, expertly, back and forth, like windshield wipers. She towelled me dry and straightened me in her chair. Again her brow furrowed. She reached for her instruments of the trade, the trowels used for foundation, the slanted blonde-hair brushes used for the brow bone, the small dainty ones used to line the lips. "Can you make my eyes look like yours?" I asked. Hers were drawn wide with liner that lifted to cat's tails at the corners. Very Anouk Aimée.

As she powdered and sponged me, I felt swept away, into a fantasy of transformation. A *parisienne* at long last. It crossed my mind that she would expect me to pay for this boudoir of beauty. She kept on telling me that I looked radiant now, *radieuse*. But I didn't need it. Or did I? Well, if it was just a small jar. Maybe there was a gift with purchase. That would make it feel like a bargain. Two for one. Oh, but I should just relax. It was just money. After I had spent it, I would never even remember that I had had it.

But it was quite a lot of money, in the end. My seductive saleslady had written down a number that looked like 2,500 French francs. It glared menacingly at me from a piece of paper that I was to take to the nearby cash register. In Paris department stores you never get the goods in hand before you pay. I thought it was an error, or that the soft and flattering beauty-counter lighting was playing tricks on my eyes. But no. That was the price. I did some rudimentary arithmetic, furtively moving my fingers as I counted. Math had never been my strong suit. Holy smokes! Even if I was off a bit, 2,500 francs ended up being almost $400! A sum far greater than any of the fancy hotel rooms I had been eyeing earlier that day.

My saleslady eyed me expectantly. She said that everything was *absolument necessaire*—the firming neck gel, the eye sculptor—"to reduce madame's puffiness"—the hydrating day cream, and, la pièce de résistance, the absolute skin-recovery serum. It looked disconcertingly like semen. "I think it is not what I need," I stammered.

"Madame?"

My lady of the gardenias was no longer smiling. In Paris, one doesn't need, one takes what one wants. That is what her impatience said to me. She turned to a second guardian of French beauty, also in an immaculate white coat, standing next to her behind the counter. I believed they were talking about me now, I was sure of it, in agitated French. They both rolled their eyes. The colleague walked away. My lady looked at me, forcing a frown. *"Ne l'aimez-vous pas?"* she frowned, thrusting a handheld mirror into my face.

She had fallen back into French, as if showing me who was who. "Do you not like it all?" I looked. I wasn't as ashen as when I had first walked in. I took the paper she was holding and walked toward the cash register. I thought that maybe I should duck into the hosiery department, get lost among the fishnets. I wouldn't need to return to La Samaritaine any time soon. I could make a run for it. But when I turned back to see if she was watching me, she was, and she waved, holding in her other hand a beribboned package loaded with my new French necessities. When I returned with the stamped receipt, she wished me, tra-la-la-la-la, a very nice *bonne soirée*. She had turned her attentions to another woman eyeing herself critically in the mirror. She had freed me to wander off again, on my own. I headed back out on to the street, clutching my purchases, and walked the distance to Tova's apartment, my face as shiny as the cold and distant moon.

ON FRIDAY MORNING I had packed my bags again, moving from Tova's apartment and into the Henri IV. The cold hadn't abated. If anything, it had gotten worse. I had spent most of the day before sitting in cafés, eating cake, waiting for nightfall, when it would be time to sleep again. The waiting was soon to be over. Stefano's train was due to arrive just after one o'clock in the afternoon. It was noon. There wasn't time to walk to Gare de Lyon. I hopped on the metro and arrived almost half an hour early, my heart heavy with fear and expectation. The station was on that day littered with heroin addicts, alcoholics, and other sorry specimens of human weakness, some twisted by deformities, others slumped, heavy with hopelessness, against the walls. Cardboard signs told mini tales of human tragedy. *"Je suis un père qui ne peut pas nourrir ses enfants. Si vous aimez Dieu, svp, aidez-moi."* I am a father who cannot feed my children, please, if you love God, help me. The arrivals board whirred rapidly above my head, white letters against a black background announcing the trains about to slide into the station from various destinations. The words filled me with wanderlust: Geneva, Marseilles, Milan, Rome. My gut twisted and turned when I saw the announcement for Zurich. Platform number four. I started to run. What if I couldn't find Stefano in the mess of voyagers disgorging from the train? I pushed past the backpackers and the businessmen with their briefcases. I took several stairs at a time.

I wondered, when I saw him, would I feel that stab of recognition that people in love always say happens when faced with the one? But when the crowd on the platform parted and I saw him standing there, looking bewildered, not knowing which way to turn for the exit, I knew in an instant that I had made a mistake.

He was no longer tan, no longer glowing like an Adonis. He had long ago left sunny Italy to move back to boring old Switzerland and was now a working stiff like me. A selfless job—caring for elderly, mentally challenged patients, spoon-feeding them, giving them sponge baths. Maybe it was penance for having led the sensual life? He had never felt comfortable about selling his body, and now he was making up for it by tending to the bodies of others. He was not highly remunerated, I could see. How good he was. I understood, but also didn't want to. I was all go-girl attitude. I wanted to be busy, happening, on the move. I coldly analyzed the situation. I noticed the frayed collar of his salt-and-pepper tweed coat. The high-pitched, nervous laugh. Girly. I had forgotten. We kissed. Nothing.

His hand was clammy, clutching mine. He lit a cigarette, and then said something in German before correcting himself. He said he didn't have an opportunity to speak much English anymore. "I am forgetting my words. But you will teach me, no?"

I walked quietly beside him, out of the station. I did not know what to say and was painfully aware that I spoke a foreign language. I was conscious of every clunky syllable, every flat vowel. On the metro we looked at each other and smiled. Shyly. He had come to me out of a belief that I was worth waiting for. I had come to him wanting to revive a more innocent past. We were both deluded. Both, I thought, noticing the faraway look in his eyes, disappointed. Inspired by my recent visit to La Samaritaine, I was wearing too much makeup. I felt him quietly scrutinizing the eyeliner, the thick layer of foundation. He had noticed that I was different. I babbled on, trying to fill the silence between us with words, fluttering gestures, anything. He listened, but I didn't think he could follow me.

We disembarked at the Pont Neuf metro station, and I led him onwards toward the Place Dauphine and the beaten-up hotel that I thought still might unite us, somehow, in a shared feeling of nostalgia. He liked relics. He drew them in his letters. And that's what our love affair was, a thing from the past honored on this trip to Paris. But the hotel's threadbare accommodations shocked him. He went to sit on a rickety chair, but it broke. "You can't be serious?" he said, confronting my folly with his clearly enunciated but heartbreaking words. He said he wanted to wash his hands, but the room didn't have hot water. "I am Swiss," he said. "We are not used to such things." I remembered that I had always known we were different. We didn't even like the same music. I wondered if he would say it. That I was crazy. But he was too polite.

"I am sorry," I said. "Shall we change hotels?" I really wanted to say, "Shall I leave?" He had come all this way to see me. I could go back to Tova's. I had an out. But then I thought it was better to stay until he left again for Zurich in two days' time. It would have been cruel to do otherwise.

We stood awkwardly facing each other. Our winter coats were still on. I thought that maybe we should have sex. To see if that might reignite something. So I initiated. He was repelled. I had pulled down his fly and was on my knees. He cupped his crotch. Yes. I felt very foolish now. I was playing so many roles that I had lost sight of myself.

We lay quietly beside each other on one of the beds, fully clothed. It creaked. I felt the coils pressing into my flesh. He lit another cigarette. The hours passed. He fell asleep. I think I did, too. I opened my eyes and saw that the room had grown darker and that Stefano was in a corner of the room, watching me. I asked him if he was hungry. Yes, he said dolefully. I followed him down the stairs and out into the night.

I had seen his worn wallet, torn at the seams. I wouldn't let him convince me to have couscous in the Latin Quarter. The occasion called for something more exciting. More expensive. My treat.

I took Stefano's hand, and we walked a short distance until I saw a short solid man methodically sweeping the sidewalk outside a fruit-and-vegetable store. I assumed the *marché* was his. Under a red awning were oranges and coconuts and lemons, tropical delicacies that stood out in vivid contrast to the wintry pallor of the surrounding street. The produce was piled high in a pyramid, making me think how patient and proud the store owner must be. How conscientious. I had a hunch that he would know a restaurant where we could go, an insider place, not a tourist trap, perhaps a place that he sold his delicious-looking fruit to, an establishment of quality? I asked him in French to give us a suggestion. He kept his head bowed for a moment, fixated on a piece of ice that refused to be uprooted from the sidewalk in front of him. I was growing desperate. I needed levity. My life depended on a fun night out.

The man looked up at me then. He looked at Stefano, glum and chain-smoking. He quietly sized us up. Thinking. And then, after about a minute, he said, *"Bon!"* He had it. A really good place. We wouldn't be sorry. He wrote the address down on the back of Stefano's book of matches.

We climbed into a taxi and were off. "Paris by night!" I said. I was trying to make the best of it. I told myself I was on a Paris adventure. Going where fate would guide me. No wrong turns, as long as you have an open mind. I told myself to enjoy the mystery ride. I whispered into Stefano's ear, as if we were lovers.

I was confused when the taxi stopped. The Rue Mazarine looked deserted. No people. No crowds. There was no indication that we had arrived in the vicinity of an "in" spot. Before us was a restaurant set back a bit from the street, partially hidden behind a series of small evergreens in painted plant boxes. The address was written large on a brass plate. It was definitely where we were supposed to be. Perhaps it was closed. I noticed a braided silk rope. I thought that if I pulled on it, someone might come. I pulled. A small metal grill on the door lifted from the inside. A pair of dark eyes. First on me, then on Stefano. I was asked what I wanted. *"Pour manger,"* I replied. The grill slammed shut—odd. Then I heard the unlocking of latches, and the door opened, slowly.

A black man in a tuxedo appeared. Very tall, very beautiful. The white of his collar highlighted the ebony lustre of his skin. He made a small bow, inviting us to enter. The room had rounded ceilings, like a cave. There were a few patrons. People nodded in our direction. Okay. Cool.

A short middle-aged woman wore a patch over an eye and walked with a rhinestone-encrusted cane. *"Monsieur. Madame,"* she said, bending her head of pink hair in our direction. She ushered us across the floor of the restaurant to a small round table covered in white linen. It was raised on a small platform—we were on display. I could go with that. I fluffed my hair and licked my lips. That was more like it, I thought, back at center stage. I told Stefano I was ravenous, simply ravenous. I perused the heavy leather menu. Excellent wine list, I said, wanting Stefano to know how cosmopolitan I was. Stefano ordered the spaghetti bolognese, the least-expensive item on the menu. He didn't know yet that I was paying. "Champagne?" I said. I wanted to be extravagant, to put the Henri IV behind me.

He giggled. Okay. Two glasses. Then two more. Finally we were talking; the fiasco had been averted.

It was close to midnight now, and the restaurant had filled with people. The black man working behind the bar was busily trying to keep up with the crush of orders. The evening had turned velvet. A trio of jazz musicians played "It Never Entered My Mind." Glasses clinked. Voices rose and fell on the cadences of animated conversation. I needed to use the ladies'. I wobbled a bit on my feet when I stood up, but then sashayed in time to the music to the back of the restaurant—and that's when I noticed. There were men in dresses, women in ties. Women with women. Lots of women. The bartender? Looked again. Not a he. A she. I went into the washroom and splashed cold water on my face.

"Stefano!" I leaned in to him across the table after I had returned, gingerly, to my seat. "Look around you." I was whispering, but probably too loudly. I gestured with my hands, making a whirling motion. I was trying to tell him that it was all mixed up. Things weren't as they seemed. He looked at me, confused. "Dyke bar," I said. "We're in a bloody dyke bar." I hoped I didn't have to translate that. But he seemed finally to understand me. He looked around the room, turning flamboyantly in his chair to make sure everyone knew he was checking them out. The patrons smiled. He smiled back.

I remembered the time in Florence when Stefano had taken me at night down the alleyways that surrounded the old basilica, Santa Croce. Inside the doorways were cross-dressers with mascara-smudged eyes and frothy wigs of shoulder-length curls. They had nodded to Stefano when we had passed by, as if they knew him. I remember that he seemed proud to show me off to them. His girl. His gladiator.

Transvestite. In French, *un travesti*. Travesty. Yes. That was us. Two poorly rehearsed players struggling through a farce. Had the fruit man seen through the charade? I imagined him chuckling as we had walked away, delighted to have pushed our affair to its comical conclusion. In any event, Stefano found it funny. For the first time that night he seemed completely at ease. He took my hand in his. "They are just following their passion. They love as we love," he said. But, unfortunately, I didn't love him back. I wanted out of there. I didn't belong, not to Stefano, and not to the sisterhood, though they had served us a round on the house. *Santé.* My Paris fantasy had become a joke.

STEFANO HELPED ME get all my luggage into the taxi. He said he wanted to drive with me to the airport. I said no, but he insisted. I think that's when I got flustered and made the mistake of telling the driver to go to Orly airport when it was really Charles de Gaulle that I needed. I realized the error only when we were nearing the terminal and read the sign, and knew I had gotten things even more terribly confused.

Upset, I started shouting that we had to turn around, quick, and head in the opposite direction. I thought I was going to miss my flight. *"Calma, calma,"* Stefano said, speaking to me in Italian. I told him to shut up, to leave me alone. All the pent-up emotion of the last few days came pouring out of me like hot lava. I instantly regretted being so explosive. It was all a big stupid mess. I said sorry. What else could I do? He said nothing. The silence in the cab was deafening.

The taxi driver drove like a fiend and got me to Charles de Gaulle with minutes to spare. I ran to the gate, Stefano running behind me with my luggage, sweating, panting. The airport personnel told me to hurry. *"Vite!"* I scrambled over to security and then realized that this was it. I would never see him again. But it was too late; I was being pushed through the door. I turned to look at him. I swear he was crying. I shouted at him from over my shoulder, good-bye.

On the plane I strapped myself into my window seat and asked the attendant for the day's newspapers. I folded them into the pocket in front of me. The plane nosed into the air, piercing through the clouds. Paris faded into the distance. I took out my Walkman and popped in a tape by Madonna. "Material Girl." I turned up the volume, much to the irritation of the portly businessman next to me. I bopped in my seat, willfully frivolous. I sang along. This could be my anthem, I thought, trying not to think of the pleading look on Stefano's face.

A month or so later I heard from him again. Another wispy letter from far away. I was back in the newsroom, churning out the bylines, working the phone. I took a moment to read the handwritten script. "In Paris we had only a bad time. It will pass. I am waiting for eternity," he wrote.

This time I picked up the phone to call him. "Stefano," I said. "Don't."

FOUR

Daughter

· 1986 ·

AFTER I LEFT Paris in February, the city went through a series of cataclysmic changes. Bombs exploded in the streets, and scores of people were wounded and in some cases killed during the blood-soaked Paris spring. The series of indiscriminate terrorist attacks was said to be linked to France's military presence in the Middle East. In March, though a bomb was diffused on the third level of the Eiffel Tower and another inside the Châtelet metro station, others exploded inside a Left Bank bookstore and in the Forum des Halles underground shopping arcade, injuring dozens of people. Violence was in the air. That same month bombs also exploded in a TWA jetliner over Greece, killing four Americans, and in a West Berlin nightclub frequented by U.S. servicemen. In April Reagan ordered retaliatory air strikes against Libya, saying the Libyan leader, Mu'ammar al-Gadhafi, was behind recent attacks against Americans. In solidarity, France in the meantime expelled four Libyan diplomats from Paris, an act that seemed only to increase the number of bombs wracking havoc on the city. In early July a car bomb blew out windows in a five-storey building on the same street that housed the French Foreign Ministry offices. No one was injured. But a few weeks later another bomb ripped through the offices of the police-run Anti-gang Brigade in central Paris, on the Quai des Orfèvres, killing one man and wounding eighteen.

I read the majority of these stories in the pages of the *International Herald Tribune*, one of several foreign newspapers regularly delivered to *The Globe and Mail* in Montreal, where my editor had shipped me that summer to fill in for the cultural bureau chief, who was off on a book leave. The paper had rented me an apartment in the city, and in the mornings I walked to the office on the top floor of a turn-of-the-century building with a wall of west-facing windows overlooking Mountain Street and the blue expanse of the St. Lawrence River. I had no friends in Montreal, and work became my refuge. I commanded my desk sometimes well into the night, filing stories, reading the wires, and scouring the piles of newspapers delivered daily to the door to stay abreast of world events, Paris increasingly being front-page news.

Daily reports of the killing and maiming in the French capital made me wonder all over again at how dangerous a city Paris was, with violence simmering just below its surface beauty. The entire city, I was learning, was on edge. No one knew where the next bomb was going to explode. But my year and a half at a top-ranking newspaper had made me fearless. After reading about these latest assaults, I picked up the phone and dialled the *Tribune* in Paris, asking to be put through to the editor in chief, Walter Wells. I figured there was plenty of work there for a journalist like me. Besides, I was eager for change.

Although wonderful, my *Globe and Mail* job had lately made me think of being elsewhere. For all the travel, excitement, and opportunities to develop my craft, my position at the paper was insecure. I was on a renewable contract, paid by the piece instead of a full-time salary. For the past year and a half the arrangement had worked well for me. I had been prolific, and so my weekly paycheck often exceeded that of a regular staff member. But I had no paid vacation time, no benefits, no guarantees that all my hard work would eventually get me a full-time position. When I repeatedly asked my editor when he planned on bringing me fully into the fold, he always gave me the same answer. "Sorry kid, hiring freeze," he said, scratching his thinning hairline. "But don't be going anywhere. We like the thought of you being around." That wasn't enough for me. I needed to think of my future.

Wells's secretary had intercepted my call to him. When I told her I was interested in working for the paper, she advised me to fax my resume with a cover letter to the *Trib*'s offices in Neuilly. In my fax I wrote a little white lie, saying I was soon going back to Paris and could meet up for a face-to-face interview. Wells had no reason not to believe me. Within a few days he had written back, saying he had the highest regard for *The Globe and Mail* and would be happy to get together with me to discuss a possible future at the *Tribune*. It felt like a lucky break. I hadn't a real plan in hand for returning, but his letter made me start organizing my trip back to Paris in earnest. I settled on a departure in mid-September, just a few weeks off, following the end of the 1986 Toronto film festival. My contract was due to expire then. My editor had said he expected to be able to renew it for another year, but I told him I had made other plans.

In my final days in Montreal I gazed out the window, toward the mouth of the Atlantic. I worried less about terrorists and more about where in Paris I would live once I got my new job. My daydreams honed in on the fully furnished apartment overlooking the Eiffel Tower in the tony 7th Arrondissement that I had visited months earlier, on the last trip, one night when I was on my own and feeling in need of companionship. Its occupant at that time was an American businessman, a friend of a friend. The person in Toronto who had scrawled his number on a piece of paper, shoving it into my hand in advance of my departure the last time, had described Sam as a budding gourmand who loved exploring the restaurants and bistros of Paris where his company had posted him for a year, paying most of his expenses. We had met inside his beaux arts–style apartment, where he served me drinks on a silver platter in front of a fire. The Eiffel Tower twinkled just beyond picture windows draped with rich silk curtains that puddled over what looked like miles of polished hardwood floor. The apartment belonged to an elderly French widow whose habit was to rent it out, fully furnished, to foreigners who reminded her of her late husband, also an American businessman. Sam was darkly handsome and gregarious, and must have fit the bill. She gave him not just the keys to her former home, with its incomparable view, but also her long-serving maid, who still came in weekly to clean the silverware, fluff the brocade cushions.

I knew Sam's term in Paris would soon be coming to a close. I thought that perhaps I could sublet the place from him once he went back to New York. Although I had only been in it once, I remembered that it was spacious and opulent, Paris as it must look to a privileged insider. I picked up the phone at my desk in Montreal and asked Sam if he'd put in a good word for me with his landlady. He said he would, on one condition. That I'd see him again, the first night I was back in Paris. "Because I'm thinking you need to try out the bed," he teased. "To make sure it's to your liking."

I returned to Toronto from Montreal at the end of August, with less than two weeks to go until my trip. I hadn't any trouble getting a last-minute ticket. The attacks in Europe had made Americans stay away in droves. Airplanes were empty, and so were hotels. Paris, when I researched it, was going for half price. I told my mother that, when I visited her before my departure. She had always loved a bargain. It was my theme as I sat at her kitchen table, trying to have a conversation with her. But she turned her back to me as I told her about my hopes for my upcoming trip to Paris. She was in one of her moods; anger enveloped her like a second skin. She had lately been gambling on the real estate market, her latest get-rich scheme. Her nerves were raw from worrying about foreclosures. But she didn't say that. She didn't say anything. Her aggressive body language did all the talking while I raved about the city.

"I've always said you should see Paris, haven't I? There are chestnut trees. Flowers on every street corner. And the museums. You'd love the museums."

She was opening and closing cupboards, loudly. She couldn't remember where she had put the scissors. She was cursing under her breath.

"The biggest is the Louvre," I continued, raising my voice to make her pay attention. "And it's next to the

Tuileries Gardens, an enormous and beautiful park unlike any you've seen, filled with fountains and statues and men in berets making crêpes, people in the latest fashions." I was selling her a postcard version of Paris, not the Paris in the headlines.

"You think me stupid, or something?" She glared at me, hands on hips.

"Let me finish," I said hurriedly. "The Tuileries Gardens."

She turned her back to me again.

"The Tuileries Gardens," I repeated, shouting above the clashing of utensils in drawers. "They have these conical trees, sculpted, not at all like our trees. Reined in."

"Stunted, you mean."

"No, lovely, and, well, let me finish, and at night you go walking and see men sitting on a wall camouflaged by them, dangling their feet, waiting for love, for a love adventure, behind the trees. Paris is like that, places where love happens." What I was trying to say was, come to Paris, love what I love, love me.

The clatter stopped. She faced me, seizing the scissors that had been eluding her these few minutes.

"All right," she said.

"All right, what?" I said.

"I'm coming."

"Coming where?" I felt my stomach pitch and dive, blindfolded, into the depths of my being.

"To Paris."

I stared, dumbstruck. I didn't think she would do it. But more to the point, I didn't think she'd do it then. "Um, you know that I am supposed to be meeting um, that guy I told you about, um, Sam? That I am supposed to, um, stay at his apartment?"

"I'm nobody's third wheel, I'll have you know," she responded, sharply. "I'll get my own hotel room. Do Paris on my own. Don't you be thinking to be taking care of me."

"Do Paris on your own?" I exclaimed. "But you don't even speak the language!"

"Before you were born, young lady, I was in London on my own. I managed there. I think it will be fun bombing around Paris by myself. I'll rent a car."

"You can't drive in Paris!" I protested. "The driving there is treacherous!"

"You organize your trip," she said, slamming a cupboard with a kick of her foot. "And I'll organize mine."

True to her word, she stubbornly organized her upcoming trip without consulting me. In the phone book she found a Toronto travel agency specializing in trips to France, and thought it better to seek the advice of a woman squeezed behind a desk in a downtown office, instead of me. She also didn't ask me what to pack and so, when the time came, packed almost everything in her closet into four large suitcases plus a carry-on. She didn't ask me many questions about Paris at all, except for the details of my flight so that, on the plane ride over, we could sit together. I meanwhile telephoned Sam and told him of the change in plans. I wouldn't stay with him, but with my mother, in a hotel of her choice. He insisted we still rendezvous the first night and also the second, given that it would be the weekend. He said he wanted to meet my mother. He was organizing a night on the town. A threesome. My mother fussed for a few days about what she should wear ignoring all my suggestions. We took a night flight to Paris and sat next to each other in the dark, barely speaking.

FROM THE AIRPORT we took a taxi to the Left Bank hotel she had booked. It was tucked away behind Saint-Séverin, one of the most beautiful churches in Paris, in the Latin Quarter. Situated near the lively Boulevard Saint-Michel, a hub for students attending the nearby Sorbonne, it was a good location if you were young, but hardly desirable if you were middle-aged and wanting sleep. As my mother quickly discovered.

She had booked a corner room on the ground floor, and the streets on both sides roared with the most ferocious traffic. I had never known Paris to be so noisy. Motor scooters ripped past, hauling hearts into throats. The bedroom held two double beds and a writing desk. The bed's coverlet was the knotty rayon kind that you see in cheap hotels everywhere. It looked worn and wrinkled. She sat down on it, and the bed seemed to sink with the weight of her disappointment. A television was mounted on the wall over the minibar. Soon after entering the room for the first time, my mother turned it on. I had never watched television in Paris before, and it shocked me. The screen showed images of Paris streets on fire. There were police cars and cordons and batons and blood. The telecast was in rapid-fire French. I could clearly make out the word *terroriste*. There must have been another bomb. But that's not what bothered me; it was that my mother had turned on the TV at all. Instinctively, like an old habit. This was not what one did in Paris—one did not replicate the customs of home. In Paris, one started afresh.

"You watch too much television," I said, my voice dripping with disapproval.

"I do not," she replied matter-of-factly. She had lain down on the coverlet, her legs stretched out before her, and she continued watching the screen.

"Why do you have it on when you don't understand a word of what's being said?"

In the silence that stretched between us, I heard my echo. I sounded intolerant and patronizing.

"It relaxes me," she said, her voice steady but defiant. She aimed the converter at the screen and turned up the volume. A scooter zipped past the window.

I retreated into a sulk. It was morning, but she said she was too tired to go out and explore Paris right away. She suggested we both get some sleep, and rolled fully clothed on to her side, her back to me once more.

I had been sleeping only a short time when the phone rang. It was Sam, calling from Paris. Oh, but I was in Paris. I forced myself to focus. We were supposed to meet for dinner, Sam said. Dinner. I hadn't even had breakfast yet. My mother stirred next to me. "What is it?" she asked.

"My date," I hissed. She laid her head back on the pillow. In Paris time it was past five o'clock in the afternoon. Sam wondered if I could be ready in an hour. I cupped the receiver and asked my mother if it was okay if I left her alone. She had said on the way over that she had no interest in going out with me, with him, that first night, saying she was no one's third wheel. Still, I didn't like the thought of leaving her alone. But she held her ground, or rather her pillow.

"Of course," she replied, sounding suddenly awake. "It's why you're here, isn't it?"

I took a bath, hoping to wash away my fatigue. I had brought a black velvet dress for my evening out. I hung it up on the back of the bathroom door to let the steam from my bath smooth away its suitcase wrinkles. A tip I had read in a fashion magazine—how to look chic after a transatlantic flight, or something like that. Except I wasn't feeling chic. Getting ready for a man I barely knew felt like a chore. I dried my hair and applied my makeup. I looked at myself in the hotel-room mirror. The face looking back at me felt foreign.

Sam stood in the lobby with a black umbrella in one hand, a briefcase in another. It was Friday, and he had just come from work. In his pin-striped suit he looked more strictly controlled than I remembered. His round face was the color of the raincoat he had folded neatly over one arm. Both his brows and mustache were thick and black, dispelling any impression of blandness. His lips were thin, but his smile amiable and easy. When he saw me, his brown eyes danced. He dropped his briefcase with such a bang that it caused the woman behind the counter to utter a tiny scream. He reached out a hand to grasp mine. I saw the glint of his cufflinks, the stark whiteness of his cuff. His grip was strong, eager. An American in Paris, not afraid of a thing. "Hi," he said enthusiastically.

He started walking out the door, expecting me to follow. I did. He walked briskly, and I had to hurry to keep pace. He asked me about my flight, about the weather in Toronto, about my hotel room. A siren wailed past us, a police car with blue lights flashing. I saw people rushing past. Sam grabbed my elbow, and continued walking. "We're going to have a great night," he said determinedly. "As luck would have it, your street has a restaurant that I've been dying to try." He came to a stop in front of a small bistro with large windows topped by an emerald-green awning. He pushed the door open for me and we entered a small, wood-panelled room that had just one other couple in it. The proprietor seated us in a booth so deep that my legs dangled.

"I heard the food here is to die for," Sam said, cracking open the menu. "I suggest we start with *soupe aux choux,* which is cabbage soup," he said. "I'm going for the *soufflé au fromage,* which is made with cheese, but you should have the *poulet de Bresse au vinaigre,* which is chicken in a wine-vinegar sauce."

I had put my menu down to watch him. Was he purposefully being condescending?

"For dessert, there's *poires à la beaujolaise.*"

"Pears poached in red wine," I said, cutting him off. His face flamed red.

"Why didn't you stop me?" he asked.

"You didn't give me the chance," I said.

"I feel foolish," he muttered. "I forgot that Canadians are bilingual."

"Well, some of us are," I said. "I'm not. But I can read a menu."

"How many times have you been to Paris, anyway?"

"This is my fourth time," I answered. "But it's the first time I'm here with my mother."

"There is so much I don't know about you," he said.

"I know," I said. And then he leaned across the table to kiss me.

He suggested that we take an eau-de-vie at his place, and so after dinner he hailed a taxi, and we went across Paris, passing through two police barricades to reach his apartment, whose large windows framed the Eiffel Tower.

Soon to be mine, I thought. I was sleepy and yawning as he took me by the hand to show me the bedroom, with a queen-sized bed overhung with a portrait of the Madonna on the wall. In the dim light of the velvety room I also saw a crucifix and a portrait of the Pope. "They freak me out," said Sam, raising an eyebrow in the direction of the icons. "I'm Jewish, but I have to sleep with them every night."

My eyes were heavy, and my head light. With the mother of God looking down at me, I forgot all about my own mother, alone in her hotel room. I didn't remember her until the next day, when the phone rang. I blinked into the darkness. Where was I? A man's voice. I listened hard. Oh yes, Sam—I was at his apartment. In Paris. Where I was with my... *Holy shit!* My mother! I listened carefully to what Sam was saying.

"Yes. I look forward to meeting you, too," he said with laughter in his voice.

What time was it? I had to know.

Sam tiptoed into the room, his steps muffled by thick carpeting. "Oh, so you're awake!"

He flew to my side, wanting to kiss me. I pulled away; I wanted to get out of the bed. I saw that I was naked. What happened last night? I could barely remember, but no need to be rude. "Um, good morning."

"Afternoon," Sam said, correcting me as he bent to nibble on my bare shoulder.

"Excuse me? Afternoon? Really? Please. What time *is* it?" I shuddered to imagine the answer.

"It is," said Sam, lifting a wrist on which was a sparkling silver-plated watch, "one o'clock exactly." He leaned in to kiss me again.

I inhaled sharply, a note of horror sounding inside my throat.

"Don't worry," Sam said cheerily. "I just spoke to your mother. You never told me she was such a crack-up!"

I sat on the edge of the bed, trying to cover myself with a sheet. I wondered how she had gotten Sam's number. I remembered that I had left my day timer behind in the hotel room. She must have searched through it. I saw her in my mind's eye, turning the pages, frantic, and I felt terribly guilty. I must get back to her straightaway. Sam told me to sit pretty; he'd made coffee.

He left the room to get it, and I jumped out of the bed and looked for my clothes. They were spread around the floor. It was all starting to come back to me—the zipper on my dress becoming stuck, me forgetting to take off my shoes, his hands on my thighs. He knew me better now, I reckoned. I glanced nervously up at the Sacred Heart of Jesus. My eye fell on the closet. The door was open, revealing a wall of suits, black, charcoal, navy-blue. Just then Sam waltzed back into the room, balancing a cup and saucer. The coffee was inky black and went down like springwater. I felt a tingling inside not entirely attributable to the caffeine. Sam had grabbed my face with his hands. He asked me to stay.

"I have to go," I said, turning to pull on my pantyhose.

"Are you sure?"

"Quite sure."

"About last night," he said, his voice revving to a low rumble of desire.

"Forget it," I said, pushing him away. "Get me a taxi. You haven't a clue about my mother. Not a clue."

I sat rigidly in the backseat of the cab as it drove away from Sam's apartment of privilege, anxious about returning to my mother in her paltry hotel. It was Saturday afternoon in late September, and the air was warm and hazy. I rolled down my window. A lemon sun hung in the sky, its rays igniting into fiery brilliance the bronze lampposts and golden sculptures on the Pont Alexandre III. As I inched toward the Left Bank, the city's glow intensified. The golden tip of the obelisk in the Place de la Concorde had also caught the sun and looked like a blowtorch singeing low-lying mauve clouds and turning their borders orange. Ahead of me was Peace in her chariot, flanked by the golden figure of *Victory* on either side of her at the top of the *Arc de Triomphe du Carrousel*, gloriously burnished. Paris *was* burning. I felt a commingling of fear and awe. I thought of my desire for Paris, how it was like a long, lingering flame burning inside me. A passion fired by longing. A dream that won't die. Its beauty was a higher standard, what I wanted for myself. But who was I kidding? Paris was eternal; I was merely human.

"I'm so sorry," I blurted, tripping out of the taxi when I saw my mother sitting on the stairs of the hotel. I inwardly ducked. I expected her to verbally thrash me, right there on the street. But she looked up not for a fight. Her face at that moment seemed to carry the entire story of her years. Her skin was the color of the sidewalk, circles ringed her eyes. She had had a sleepless night, I thought.

"How was your night?" she asked, her voice curiously flat.

"Good," I said, not wanting to say anything more. "Nice guy?" she said, looking at her nails. She was picking at them, making the skin look raw.

"Very nice," I said. My heart was pounding inside my evening clothes. I felt the perspiration pooling inside the cloth. "Would you mind waiting while I change?" I asked. "Well, I've waited all day," she said. "Why should I mind now?"

I raced inside the hotel room, where the bed was neatly made. I tore off my dress and put on a skirt and a blouse, suitable attire for a quick tour of the sights. I ran back outside. I would make it up to her. I would cram it in, eight hours of sightseeing into three. We were meeting Sam for dinner in a few hours. He would come to pick us up at the hotel—but first we needed fortifications.

I whisked us into a nearby café and ordered us both a large café crème and a croissant. My mother drank thirstily. "I had tried to get a coffee by myself in the morning," she said. "But I didn't know how to count the money. Then when I needed to use the washroom, I kept saying, *la toilette! la toilette!* The looks on their faces. They thought I was daft."

I felt badly all over again, having left her to fend for herself. But I had learned over the years not to show her my vulnerabilities. With her, I became the take-charge person. A militant would-be mommy. I counted out her money and I asked her to repeat after me, *"Où est le W.C. ?"*

"Ew eh la doobley-vey say," she responded, right as rain.

"Okay, then," I pronounced. "I think we're ready to go. We've quite a bit to see before dark!"

With my mother I reduced Paris to a greatest-hits list, one played at a dizzying speed. I had long ago lost the ability to have a conversation with her, so acted like a tour guide, spouting facts and figures. Our first stop was Notre Dame. I commanded her not to look right, not to look left, but to look straight up at the famous rose window on the south facade. "It dates from the 13th century, and the rose is a symbol of the Virgin," I said pedantically. "It recurs in courtly love poetry, the art of the troubadours, who were French, you must know." But she had, perhaps wisely, tuned me out. Her focus was on an old man praying on his knees. He held a rosary in his gnarled hands and was silently counting the beads, eyes closed. A priest in white robes floated down the central aisle, wafting incense. My mother sniffed and, leaning into me, whispered, "This place reminds me of your father." I looked at her, alarmed. We never spoke about him, and I didn't think Paris was the place to start.

I nudged her in the direction of the cathedral's north tower. "We're going up," I said, and led the climb up nearly four hundred spiralling steps to the *Galerie des Chimères*, perch of the gargoyles. When we got to the top, we were both huffing and puffing. But our reward was the view— Paris as seen from heaven: still, quiet, and faraway, a city I could imagine fitting into a jewelry box. I pointed out the spire of Sainte-Chapelle. I told my mother that it was one of my favorite places in all of Paris. "See the stained glass windows, absorbing the ruby-red light?"

But my mother seemed more to like the sweep and scope of Paris, and was less interested in focusing on details, as I did. "It reminds me of Edinburgh," she said. Edinburgh was her birth city.

"It's not at all like Scotland!" I protested, shouting to make myself heard over the wind.

She shrugged her shoulders. "Is too," she said. "Just as old, with just as much history. Do you think I'm from some kind of backwater?"

"Let's go," I replied wearily, and led her back outside, toward the tiny and picturesque Île Saint-Louis, where Paris, in the form of *grands hôtels particuliers* with hidden gardens and lace-curtain windows overlooking the Seine, was magnificently unique. A crowd was lined up in front of Berthillon, the maker of luxurious ice creams and sorbets.

She assumed we'd have one. "No," I said, somewhat impatiently. "No time."

I picked up the pace, running her along the riverbank at the back end of Notre Dame, in full view of the flying buttresses. She said she needed to rest a moment, and stopped to gaze into the inky waters. A light breeze tickled her face, and a far-off look entered her eyes. I stamped my foot while I waited. I had her edification in mind. I told her we had to get going.

I led her quickly down the Rue Dauphine, past the antique gas lamps that gave Paris its other name, City of Light. This time I told her to look right, look left, and not up. "See the pointed windows? Gothic I think. And that arched doorway, so small? Must be from the Middle Ages. People were shorter then. Mind the dog poop."

We passed the Rue de l'Abbaye and continued down the narrow and winding Rue de Furstenberg, created for horses and their riders to reach the former abbey that lay hidden behind high stone walls, which still lent the street a feeling of seclusion. I knew every bend along the way, every shady bench. I used to wander it alone, savoring its faded elegance and quiet charm. I had once dreamed of sharing it with someone special. Paris was always emotional for me, but on this trip I didn't linger. It had started to drizzle, and I hurried my mother along, leading her toward Rue Jacob, with its sprinkling of fashionable boutiques hung with velvet curtains and paisley wallpaper. I knew it well, as it bled into Rue de l'Université, where I had once lived. We passed cafés and curiosity shops with stuffed birds and animal skeletons in the windows in our approach to the apartment building where I had resided, with another family, seven years earlier. The gate was open, revealing a cobblestone courtyard filled with parked Citroëns and Fiats and flower boxes spilling over with geraniums, looking just as I had left it. I peered up to the second floor, to a large rectangular window covered with a wrought-iron grille. I could see my former bedroom, and I pointed it out to her. My mother quietly took it all in. I had told her about this place so many times. She knew I had been happy there, and miserable. I wondered what she was thinking now, but didn't have an opportunity to find out. We were being pushed by pedestrians clutching big umbrellas, and a torrent of *tuts* fell about our heads. It was time to move on.

We crossed down Rue du Bac, laden with antique stores through the windows of which we could see enormous crystal chandeliers and swirling bronze statues of the dancer Loie Fuller, poster girl for French artisans of the art nouveau era. The street ended at the elegant Quai Voltaire and its row of luxury town houses on the shores of the Seine. We had been sheltered inside the labyrinthine streets of Saint-Germain, because on the Quai Voltaire the traffic was cacophonous, hitting our eardrums with startling violence. And yet the magnificence of the vista

opening before us cancelled any feeling of discomfort. Tall
poplar trees lined the riverbank, their leaves thick and
brilliantly green. A well-dressed woman clicked quickly
by on heels, pulling a coiffed white poodle on a pink
leather leash. Boats blasted their horns, chimneys soared,
and beyond was the Louvre, standing sentry, across
from us on the other side of the river. We crossed the
Seine on the elegantly arched Pont Royal, linking left
bank with right, to reach the museum. A cluster of rain-
coats clogged the entranceway. I craned my neck and
saw that it was a police check; they were opening back-
packs, inspecting purses and packages. I told my mother
she'd have to open her fanny pack. When she got to the
front of the line, she raised her hands in the air to enable
the guard to frisk her. "What did he say?" asked my
mother, turning to me.

"He said it wasn't necessary."

My mother flashed him a smile. *"Merci,"* she said, a
born flirt.

Once inside, she stared with amazement at the marble
floors and the gilded ceilings, the fluted columns and the
ornate staircase that then dominated the inner foyer. The
Winged Victory of Samothrace stood majestically at the top
of the stairs where last I'd seen her. That much was still
the same. I had one thing in particular I wanted to show
my mother, and told her to follow me, past Botticelli's
fresco of Venus and the Three Graces, their fresh faces

framed by flowers, and the armless *Venus de Milo,* up more stairs and down the center of the narrow Grand Gallery filled with Italian master paintings. Signs for *La Joconde,* what the French call the *Mona Lisa,* pointed the way. We entered the Salle des États, and there she was, darkening a far wall.

"You're kidding me," my mother said. "The *Mona Lisa.* Goddamn it. Now you're talking."

The painting looked dark and smudgy, a result of Leonardo da Vinci's shadowy application of paint. To properly see the figure, it's better to stand back, take the long view. But my mother wanted a good look and had gone up close to the painting, bending forward into it.

"Ne touchez pas."

A museum guard was at my mother's elbow, warning her not to get too close. She ambled back to me.

"It's smaller than I thought it would be," she frowned. "And I can't say I know what all the fuss is about. She's not what you'd call a beauty."

She didn't understand the painting, I thought, just as I didn't understand her.

"They say she's pregnant," she mused, after a few moments. "I remember being pregnant with you, in a dress with a square neck like the one Lisa is wearing. I came to Canada in that dress. No one knew about you, you were my secret. I ran a race when I was six months along with you. I won, too." She placed a hand on my shoulder, stopping me. She gave me a little squeeze. I felt it as a pinch and pulled away.

"We've seen enough here," I said, and headed in the direction of the French masters. We stood in front of the *Raft of the Medusa*, a portrait of a shipwreck, with people drowning, the remaining survivors calling out desperately for help, and were dwarfed by its sheer monumentality. "It's a great Romantic painting," I said. "The artist uses a pyramid shape to organize his material, including body parts, into a well-balanced whole. Can you see that?"

"Jesus Murphy," said my mother. "You know a lot, don't you?"

She sauntered over to Delacroix's dramatic *Liberty Leading the People*, leaving me to stew in my sophistic juices. I felt she was being unfair. She's the one who had always insisted I be the best, the brightest, the fastest. "You have to win the race," she used to tell me as she signed me up for kiddie races at church picnics. I was three. She stood behind me at the starting line, whispering strategies. "Ready, steady, go!" I ran like the wind, my dress opening. My mother had sprinted ahead to catch me, her arms open at the finish line. I sailed right into them, eager for her embrace. "Good girl!" she said. "You did it. You were first." I wanted to give back to her what she had given me, if only to lessen the guilt I felt for being the one who took the prize. Because it had come at a cost. She had driven me so hard she had driven me away from her, driven us apart. In Paris,

I had hoped we could find some common ground. But I realized that I was going about it the wrong way. I wasn't sharing Paris with her. I was shoving it down her throat.

I caught up with her. She had wandered off on her own and was standing in front of the 16th-century painting of the Duchesse de Villars pinching the nipple of her sister, Gabrielle d'Estrées. It was a strange painting, and I admit I have never understood it. Still, I was irked by the way my mother pointed and smirked at it. The upward roll of her eyes. "What's going on there?" said my mother with an ah-get-on-with-ya kind of scoff. I refused to answer. I had been wishing for her to suspend disbelief, somehow. But it wasn't working.

We exited in front of the Palais Royal. It had stopped raining, and the sun was radiant in the sky. My mother squinted at me and said she was starving. "Let's get some fries. French fries," she smiled, emphasizing the word French. "That's funny, don't you think?" I fought the lump rising in my throat. When she wanted to laugh, I wanted to cry. We were polar opposites. Resigned, I asked her where she wanted to go. "I can see the *Arc de Triomphe*," she said, puffing her cheeks as she said it, drawing out the "f" sound, trying to make me laugh. "Let's walk up the Champs-Élysées. I need some air. I've had about all the culture I can take."

We merged with the Saturday crowd, strolling delight-edly on the wide sidewalks of the grand avenue edged by chestnut trees. She smiled contentedly, sunshine brightening the fake blonde in her naturally brown hair. She started to sing. "April in Paris, chestnuts in blossom, holiday tables under the trees." When I was younger, when friends came over and heard her singing from inside another room, they'd ask me if the radio was on. That's how dulcet her singing voice was, and how very different from her everyday speaking voice, which boomed and was generally devoid of softness. So it should have comforted me. I had grown up listening to her break into song all my life—but that was the problem: I wanted my life to be different. It was singing at the wrong time, in the wrong place. It sounded the wrong note.

As we continued to meander up the "triumphal way," as the French call it, we settled into an uneasy silence. Finally we neared the *Arc de Triomphe*. "I want you to take my picture," she said. She positioned herself next to one of the avenue's art nouveau streetlights. I had to step backwards into the advancing crowd to get her fully in the frame. She had climbed up onto the base of the light, standing head and shoulders above me, smiling giddily into the camera. "Pa-ree," she said, instead of cheese.

We crossed to the other side of the Champs-Élysées, and I led her to Fouquet's, almost as much of a Champs-Élysées landmark as the *Arc de Triomphe*. Its wine-red awning, with the celebrated bistro's name etched in gold, shaded cane chairs, and small circular marble-topped tables lining an outdoor terrace. There were slim-hipped women with long, shiny hair, wearing large dark sunglasses as they gingerly sipped their espresso. They looked as if they had all the time in the world with which to indulge the time-honoured Paris ritual of sitting outdoors and watching the fashion parade stroll by.

An older gentleman with a tuft of gray hair and a periwinkle-blue suit was also on the terrace. He kept checking a gold watch that hung by a chain from his vest pocket. Time had run out for him. He stood up from his table and made a slight bow in the direction of my mother, who was obviously still a head-turner where men were concerned. I could see the allure. She was different from Parisian women, fuller through the hips and thighs, with an ample bosom and a bottom round as a pillow. *"Madame,"* he said, offering her his seat. She wiggled in his direction, sliding into the chair as he held it gallantly for her. *"Merci,"* she cooed. He walked away, disappearing into the crowd. My mother wiggled again, this time in her seat. "I can see why you like it here," she said with a knowing smile and a twinkle in her eye. She was suddenly acting like a girlfriend, chattering away, touching my arm, light as a balloon.

I didn't understand her, so concentrated instead on the waiters. They were familiar to me. They were the same men in white, full-body aprons, indentured to a life of service. I had encountered them the last time I was in Paris and every time before that. I was sure I would meet them time and again. They were one of the constants in Paris, and in the stolid way they carried on their time-honoured métier, carrying cups of coffee, wiping down tables, they seemed to shore up the city's shifting emotional landscape with a sense of permanence.

Sitting and observing, not walking and talking like a tour guide, I absorbed the regulating rhythm of the facades, all uniformly white, an ordered idea of beauty. It didn't matter what shape they were. Square, rectangle, or triangle—as was the case for those buildings that plowed into street corners like the noses of schooners out on the high seas—the multiplicity of buildings serving a variety of purposes, from residences to restaurants, united themselves behind a singular but massive architectural style.

Then I looked over at my mother relishing her hamburger and *frites*. I nursed a Perrier with lime and wondered if we could ever be similarly united. The word family never stuck well with us. There was little cementing us other than blood and personal history, however rocky. Is that what made us want to cleave, the mere fact of being mother and daughter? Other than that, what did we have in common, she in her blue jeans, me in my tight-fitting skirt? How would we bridge the gap that years of hurt and indifference had wedged between us?

Boom! A loud explosion. The pigeons rose and fell with the bang. When they hit the cement again they did a panicked circle dance, their necks craning, their eyes bugging out of their heads. They resembled us, or we them. No one knew what was going on. People were half standing up, half sitting down. Everyone was running for cover—except for the waiters. They were cleaning the tables, miffed that people had left without paying. Surly words. Gallic shrugs.

Panicked, I struggled for control. "Mother!" She had just seconds ago been enjoying a glass of red wine. "I think it's a bomb!" I snapped. "Now stop your drinking! We have to make a run for it!"

My mother told me to take it easy. Or so I thought I heard her say. Her words were drowned out by the loud wail of sirens screaming up and down the Champs-Élysées. I grabbed her hand, aware that I hadn't held it in a long time. I pulled her out of her chair and begged her to hurry.

We soon found out that the blast had occurred less than a block from where we had been sitting, in the Renault car dealership on the Champs-Élysées. People were running and yelling. A large crowd was forming close to where the blast had just occurred. My mother wanted to stop and take a look. She slipped from my grasp. I rushed after her. I saw shattered glass on the avenue and an upturned car. A woman was screaming, her face and hands covered in blood. An ambulance skidded to make a turn right in front of us, and I had to pull my mother back lest she become another casualty. Gendarmes in their soup-can caps whistled loudly at us, and other rubber-neckers who had similarly stopped to look for signs of gore. They waved at us, hands quarantined behind white gloves, ordering us to move along. I didn't understand what had happened. Had there been a bomb? Or a car crash? I heard the crowd saying, as if one, the word *terroriste*. I told my mother we would be better off taking the metro back to the hotel. I was trying mentally to change channels. "Sam's picking us up at seven," I said. "You'll have just enough time to take a bath."

WE STOOD, THE three of us, in front of Le Procope, the oldest coffeehouse in Paris, in Saint-Germain. We had wandered there after our meal at the Alsatian restaurant where Sam had made reservations. The food was heavy and northern, full of garlic sausages and oiled potatoes, not my favorite fare, but my mother enjoyed it. How had he known? We had been walking, to burn off the apple cake served with prune eau-de-vie. I had let them walk ahead, arm-in-arm. I saw how she looked at him, grinning. She had had few chances in life, I thought. There was a puddle in the street that my mother was about to step into, wearing her strappy gold sandals with the open toes. But Sam, at just the right moment, lifted her at the waist and carried her slightly aloft. She laughed out loud and seemed almost to dance in the air before touching back down on the cobblestone street. I was so genuinely happy in that moment, so deeply relieved. If Sam had thought that being nice to my mother would make me think more positively about him, he had calculated correctly. I liked him, liked his character. He was good; he treated my mother as something precious, something worthy. It was what I had wanted to do but couldn't. Each time I thought of showing her affection, I tripped over and became entrapped by my hurt. He could enjoy her, and was the perfect gentleman.

THE NEXT DAY was my interview with Walter Wells. I hadn't slept well because my mother and I had had a fight. I spent the night sleeping in the bathtub. When I looked in the mirror, my eyes were puffy, my skin chalky. I was upset with my mother and already blaming her for sabotaging my big day.

The *Tribune*'s offices were in Neuilly, a Paris suburb, and housed in a plain modernist office tower that would have been more at home in Toronto or New York than in Paris. I took a deep breath as I pushed through the front doors. The lobby was hushed. But after exiting an elevator that took me up to Wells's office, inside the newsroom I hit a wall of noise. The ricochet of fingers pounding on keyboards, phones ringing, radios blaring, voices exploding on the air. That morning another bomb had gone off in the city, outside a department store in a working-class neighborhood. Women and children had been hurt. Wells and his colleagues had their hands full cranking out the latest story about the attack on Paris.

I waited for nearly thirty minutes to see him. He eventually burst in on the waiting room, a blaze of energy, and apologized profusely for having kept me waiting. Ushering me into his office, he sat behind his desk and folded his hands before him, ready to give me his undivided attention. His eyes shone with kindness. He had a full head of wavy hair and a chin-hugging beard that lent him an avuncular air. I realized then that I had no reason to be nervous. He was a gentle and inquisitive man, full of courtesy and tact as he leafed through my articles, actually reading a few straight through, his perusal of them sometimes punctuated by a snort of a hmmm. I interpreted the noise as a sign of some kind of interest in me.

He leaned back in his chair when he was through. "I know of your paper," he said. "Excellent reputation. A writers' paper, is it not?"

I told him that I was surrounded by great writers, yes, but that I hoped to work now in Paris, where I believed my writing would improve—inspired, no doubt, by the city, itself.

Wells then told me about his wife, Patricia Wells, the noted food critic (I hadn't realized until then that they were related), and allowed that I had a point. "Paris does inspire, and deeply. Pat says she has the best job in the world, writing about food and writing about food in the city where it is a religion. Trust me, I understand why you want to be here. I never want to leave."

But, and this was the kicker, he didn't hire writers. He bought their words on a contractual basis. And not often. The paper's affiliation with the *Chicago Tribune* meant that he had free access to copy already paid for elsewhere.

I wondered to myself why he had asked me to come, then?

"Have you any experience copy editing?" he asked. "Your paper's reputation lies with its editors. If you can edit, I might be able to offer you a desk job."

I told him the truth. Not only did I not have any editing experience, I didn't want to be an editor. "I can't work behind the scenes," I said. "I need the spotlight." I hoped that he didn't think me arrogant; I wasn't trying to be. My desire was to express myself, make myself heard. Writing was my escape. Even a job offer in the city of my dreams couldn't make me forgo that.

Wells offered me his hand and asked me to keep in touch. "Let me know if you ever change your mind."

I left feeling despondent, but also strangely gratified. He had treated me as an equal. He had shown me respect. He had encouraged me, a stranger, as a peer on the international journalistic stage. He had allowed me my voice.

I decided to call Sam from inside the metro station. I was getting off at Concorde, the stop located near his offices, which were inside one of the stately mansions fronting the square decorated with baroque fountains commandeered by Neptune and his fat-cheeked water sprites. I doubted I would see him again, despite his saying that we would see each other more frequently once he was back in New York. I didn't want another long-distance romance. I had called to say good-bye.

"I'm going to be selfish and say that I am glad you aren't going to be working for the *Trib*," Sam said. "Maybe what you should really be thinking about is working for *The New York Times*."

"Perhaps," I answered pensively. "Perhaps."

I found my mother just where I had told her to find me, at Galignani, the English bookstore. I had arranged for us to meet there because if I was late, at least she could bide her time with some reading. She didn't ask me about my interview. I knew from experience to submit to her need to talk, to dominate the conversation, which she did at that moment with enthusiasm. She had, while I was gone, purchased our tickets for the flight to Nice. We were leaving for the Côte d'Azur the next day. "I'm fair chuffed with myself," she said, smiling broadly. "I got us booked in first class." I was taken aback, as I was supposed to have arranged the flights. It was why we were on the Rue de Rivoli, a street lined with travel agencies and money changers and small stores hawking trinkets of Paris. I marvelled that she had gone to the trouble, but I could see that it had restored her equilibrium. The take-charge person was back in charge. I swallowed my wounded pride.

"Look what else I bought." She pulled out a plastic bag with a white T-shirt emblazoned with a heart flanked on one side by "I" and on the other by "Paris." "I ♥ Paris," she roared with laughter. "The girls will love it!" She was referring to her large group of female friends back home in Toronto.

I sucked in my breath sharply, worried I'd say something that would ruin that all-too-rare moment of gaiety. But I couldn't stop myself. I was jealous that she hadn't bought anything for me. I said the T-shirt was tacky.

We left the bookstore and wandered back in the direction of Place de la Concorde. I wanted to show her the ornate excess of the fountains. I hadn't done that yet. Traffic swirled madly from several directions, and we had to cross the road. There was no stopping the cars in their speedy circular drive, but I told my mother to make a run for it. Gamely she went first, and then it was my turn.

I made it across the road, but on the Place de la Concorde the heel of my shoe caught on a cobblestone, and the skirt I was wearing was far too tight to allow me to break my fall. I saw myself tumbling forward as if in slow motion, and could do nothing to stop myself. I fell directly onto my knees. The pain was sharp.

In an instant my mother was on top of me, yanking me to my feet. Supporting me, she led me over to one of the fountains. I stumbled and fell again, against her. I was in a daze. When I looked into her face, I saw that she was frantic. She was calling out my name, her mouth wide, her teeth exposed. I could tell by the strain on her face that she was shouting, but I couldn't hear her. I couldn't hear anything. Not the violent gurgling of the water that she was splashing furiously into my face, not the rev of the cars still motoring around us, oblivious to our tiny drama unfolding at the center of their circle of hell. I had gone deaf. I even tried saying my own name to myself. Silence, such as I had never experienced before, the deep dark hush of the sea. I thought I would faint. My mother shook me. I looked at her again, confused. Her mouth opened and closed; her eyes brimmed with fire and tears. I shifted my gaze to the dolphins carved into a baroque fantasia of curving lines, then went back to the face of my mother, with deeply etched lines of her own, fissures of worry. I felt the urge to throw up, and leaned over the fountain's edge. My body heaved and my ears popped. In that instant, I could once more hear the shouting, the honking, the stop and start of the traffic. I could also hear my mother sobbing, drawing in great gulps of air as she slumped to the ground.

"Mother, mother. I'm okay. I'm okay."

"If anything ever happened to you, I'd..."

She didn't finish her sentence; she didn't need to. We were both of us on our knees, desperately holding onto each other, accidentally reunited, supported by monuments of Paris.

She wiped away her tears with her sleeve and blew her nose loudly into a piece of napkin she had found in the pocket of her leather jacket. "You pierce my heart," she said.

My falling, and the resulting shock, the reason for my temporary descent into deafness, had rocked her to the core, she said. It was as if I had dropped a bomb on her. "Look at you," she sniffed, struggling to compose herself. "So elegant. And then you fall flat on your face."

It was a strange way to discover that she did love me, after all, in return. Paris was my witness.

FIVE

Miss Lonelyhearts

· 1990 ·

SOON AFTER I returned to Toronto, *The Globe and Mail* hired me as its full-time dance critic, then the newspaper's highest-ranking writing category. It was a job I adored. I loved the challenge—criticism is hard, dance criticism harder still. Often I felt like an astronomer with a telescope, focusing on faraway detail through the narrowest of lenses, seeking out the last twinkle of phenomena no longer existing in real time. Dancers as exploding stars, gone in a twinkle of an eye, their incendiary presence more a memory of experience than experience itself. My task was to reconstruct the energy that had pushed them into being in the first place, to make their trajectories through space clear to the readers. After a performance I would pull away for the wider view, looking to connect a single source of starlight with the other brilliant dots studding the dance universe. I was also always looking for a narrative, a structure with which to tell their ephemeral stories.

You could say I was good at it. In any event, my professional peers acknowledged in me a talent for dance writing when in 1989 they nominated me for a National Newspaper Award in the category of feature writing. This category was normally the preserve of foreign correspondents and war reporters, writers of so-called hard stories. My nominated article was a piece of investigative reporting on the National Ballet of Canada. My editor at that time commended me, saying arts writing, considered soft—especially dance writing—had never before been so highly recognized. I didn't win, but went home with a citation of excellence that my mother proudly framed to hang on her wall. It was my last moment of glory. Shortly afterward, the newspaper experienced a change of guard, and with that came a sharp reversal in my fortunes.

WHEN A NEW editor arrived on the scene, I was inexplicably deemed unworthy of the dance-critic title. This new hire, a woman with no prior newspaper experience, called me an incompetent writer to my face. Merit? The idea appeared ludicrous to her. She thought me wholly unprofessional.

The newspaper was unionized, so she couldn't get rid of me just because, as she told me one day during a particularly memorable tête-à-tête in her office, "she hate[d] that insipid smile of yours." She could only fire me for cause. At first she just made life miserable for me. She axed my weekly national arts column, telling me she couldn't abide my picture logo. She got the music critic to write on dance without my knowledge, and published our articles side by side in the newspaper to let the readers, she expalined to me, see who did the better job. A colleague, then the paper's books editor, told me that she stuck her fingers down her throat when he put forward my name for writing a new column. Soon other colleagues were siding with her against me behind my back. She scrutinized my expenses. She got me to write on subjects in which I had no expertise or interest, seemingly in hopes of seeing me fail. Such punishing tactics continued for about a year, and then she believed she got me.

A month before Christmas 1990 she accused me of plagiarism.

She organized a disciplinary meeting at which I was asked to explain my repetition of a sentence from the press kit given me by the physician I had interviewed for a recent article on arts medicine, an assignment she had chosen for me several weeks before. The sentence described the role musician Leon Fleisher had played in getting arts medicine legitimized. As it was a subject I knew nothing about, I had relied on the press kit for background. At the time, arts medicine was a burgeoning field, and little else had been written on it. I said what I had done was research, not plagiarism. But none of my protests mattered.

I was suspended for almost a month without pay, and a disciplinary letter was put in my employment file warning me that any future acts of misconduct would result in instant termination. I was devastated. I had never been in trouble before. I had never even gone to the principal's office as a kid. So much was at stake—my dignity, my honor, my sense of pride. I felt branded a thief and a liar. The shame was terrible.

To make matters worse, my mother had booked herself a sunny vacation away with friends for the upcoming Christmas holidays and hadn't invited me. "You're thirty years old!" she said irritably when I asked why she had to go away.

I was left pondering her meaning. Was I too old, already, to need my mother? Not yet hardened enough to bear Christmas alone as an alienated modern-day existential entity? If not, why not? Was I that weak? My mother departed before I could come up with an answer. I felt her absence acutely.

The day she left, I sat glumly at my desk inside my downtown Toronto apartment, willing myself to write. But I had difficulty composing myself, let alone a sentence. I had been crying since morning, tears of self-pity, I admit. I felt friendless, motherless, utterly alone. Picking up my pen, I aimed it within striking range of the sheet of paper in front of me, but no words came. The lines on the page were the same tepid blue as the veins in my wrist. Lines. Veins. Lines. Veins. I put the ballpoint to my flesh. I pressed down. I made a tiny O on the inside of my left wrist. I pressed again, and again. My arm soon ulcerated zeroes. I was the zero. I stabbed faster, harder. The Os became ringed with blood. I had hurt myself. I wondered if could I die this way, poisoned by my pen? Yes. No. I was shouting at myself. My voice bounced thinly off the bedroom walls, crowding in on me.

I didn't know what to do. I didn't know how to cope. I didn't know if I could survive the disappearance from my life of the one thing that had long defined me, sustained me, and given me hope: my writing, irrevocably blemished.

That's when I remembered the letter. It was easy to find amid the papers on my desk: a wafer-thin envelope with a crooked line of oxblood stamps depicting Marianne, the bare-breasted apotheosis of the French Revolution. In the weeks that it had been in my possession, I had been using it as a makeshift coaster. It had grown stained with the rings of coffee cups. I had not taken it seriously. It was a chatty missive from Rosemarie, more acquaintance than friend, who months earlier had moved to Paris. Despite being fluently bilingual, she had had difficulty landing a job in her field of public relations. In her large loping writing style, she wrote that Paris was shutting her out, making her feel homesick and desirous of company. Any company, it had seemed when I first read her letter, as long as it was from home.

We didn't know each other well. Mainly we knew some of the same people, frequented the same parties. Essentially we were strangers, but strangers who sensed a similarly desperate need for companionship. And so I read the letter again, this time ignoring what I knew in my gut were words of insincerity: "Why don't you come to Paris for the holidays? We'll have champagne and oysters for New Year's. I know the perfect place."

I held onto that letter as if it were a lifeline. Why not? I was alone; she was, too. Together we could fill the void that was Christmas. I would tell her nothing of my troubles at work. I would act free as a bird, flying on the wings of spontaneity. The only problem was, I was broke. I had been without a salary for the last three weeks—I would barely be able to pay the rent, let alone buy an airline ticket. But maybe I had enough air miles.

I wiped away my tears and dialled Air Canada. It turned out that I did have enough points to get a last-minute ticket, business class, all that was left, to Paris. I hung up the phone, feeling already in flight, determined to leave my worries behind.

Rosemarie had probably asked everyone in her address book to make the trip over. I dialled her next, hoping I was the first desperado to have answered her call.

She answered on the seventh ring. "I hope you're not coming just to see me," she said. "I don't even have a bedroom. I sleep on the floor. I'd have nowhere to put you." I said I'd ring her right back.

No way could I afford a hotel. But I was Paris obsessed; nothing would deter me. I rang up Danielle, my old friend. She had lived in Brussels for the last few years but was back in Paris, recently married. I was in luck: she and her new American husband were going on a Caribbean vacation just after Christmas. I'd have their apartment all to myself.

"You are always welcome, you know," Danielle said, which made me feel like crying again.

I called Rosemarie back to tell her I had somewhere else to stay. It was done. I had found a way out of my misery. If Toronto wanted to ostracize me, Paris would be my refuge.

DANIELLE, DEAR DANIELLE, was waiting for me when I exited the doors of Charles de Gaulle loaded down with luggage. She smiled as soon as she saw me, her cheeks dimpling. I hadn't seen her in years. She was still pretty, in a plump sort of way, still radiated jollity. But as I moved toward her, I heard her gasp. Was it my appearance, haggard after months of distress? Or the number of bags I had brought for a relatively short ten-day visit? I had wanted to return to Paris in style, but more urgently, I had wanted to hide my shame, so I had stuffed suitcases full of fancy dresses and imitation Chanel suits that I had gotten a Toronto seamstress to knock off for me from the pages of fashion magazines.

Her newly expanded apartment was on the fifth floor of a corner building in the neighborhood named for its central landmark, the Bastille, the notorious prison. A once-seedy area, consisting of narrow laneways and squat buildings, this was where the mob, immortalized by Dickens in *A Tale of Two Cities,* had knitted their plot to behead the king.

The rabble had long since moved away. Yuppies like Danielle and her new husband, Max, had now taken over, buying up dilapidated apartments and transforming them into upscale lofts. The new inhabitants with their seemingly limitless spending power had brought with them a push toward gentrification.

When we drove up the Rue de la Roquette, I noticed a spate of new cafés and restaurants, contemporary art galleries, and freshly painted fashion boutiques. Where the prison had been, a new steel-and-glass opera house had opened its doors just the year before, on July 14, 1989, the two hundredth anniversary of the Bastille's storming.

Still, by Canadian standards the apartment was small. The kitchen was about the length of a bicycle. But Danielle's recent renovation had yielded a second bathroom as well as an extra bedroom, a home office, a reading room, and the downstairs living room where we sat mulling over our meal. Each room was small like a cell, though equipped

with such modern amenities as a Minitel computer catalog-
ing the millions of listings in the Paris phone book, a
French invention. You typed in the name of a restaurant
and it gave you the address, the telephone number, and a
brief description. I had never seen anything like it. This
was the new Paris, building itself up from the past.

"You couldn't get this much space anywhere else in
Paris," Danielle boasted. She tucked into the salad she had
made with frisée lettuce and crumbled goat cheese. "In
Paris, to get this kind of space you'd either have to inherit
an apartment of this size or else murder someone," she
said, licking her knife. She was being facetious. But her
point was that Paris real estate was at a premium.

I looked past her, out the window at her back. Space
was as tight on the outside of the apartment as on the inside.
Her building was practically squeezed up against another,
located across the street. If I had had a broom in my hand,
I could probably have toppled the pots of desiccated geraniums on the across-the-way neighbor's windowsill. As
Danielle continued to chew and contentedly swallow, I
watched as a middle-aged man moved gingerly about his
apartment, setting his own table for lunch. He poured
himself a glass of red wine and turned on the television.
He seemed to live alone. I sat for a moment, transfixed, as
I watched other strangers engaged in a variety of private
but perfectly banal acts straight through Danielle's winter-
stained windows—people combing their hair, washing

dishes, singing to a pet canary, reading a book. The impression was that Paris was a city of beehives, closely stacked together and buzzing with activity. I secretly coveted the honey inside, the sweet humanity that I hoped would soon nurture me and satisfy a growing longing for acts of kindness and shared intimacy.

I turned my attention back to Danielle. "Come on," she said. "You have to eat. Really, you've grown too thin. You're not on some kind of weird diet are you?" I thought to fess up. I was a guest in her home, after all. I started at the beginning: the changes at work, the name-calling, the reprimands, the recent three-week suspension. I spoke for a long time. Danielle sat quietly, listening. She was just then in the throes of turning herself into an independent business consultant for some of France's biggest corporations. She was business minded, sharp as a pin. I had almost flunked grade 9 math. She had always liked me regardless, calling me her artsy friend. A flake whom she found irresistible. I hoped she'd embrace me still. But she had already gotten up from the table to clear the dishes. "People don't just attack you for no reason," she said, turning to look at me from her place in the munchkin kitchen. "What did you do to piss them off?"

I tried to change the subject. I asked her what she wanted to do about Christmas, just a few days off. *"La Veille de Noël,"* she called it, referring to the night the French traditionally celebrate the holiday, December 24, Christmas

Eve. "I've never done it before." Of course. Of course. She was Jewish. I had almost forgotten. She hardly raised the topic of her religion, perhaps because she didn't come from a practicing family. Her mother was from Paris, and during the war had been in Drancy, the internment camp that held French Jews until they were deported for extermination. She had survived, moving eventually to Toronto, where Danielle had been born. She was dour where Danielle was gregarious, never smiling at me, perhaps because she caught me staring at the prisoner serial number tattooed on her arm.

Danielle must have sensed my unease. She approached me, grinning, offering a cup of coffee. "Max is Christian, lapsed, mind you, but somewhere in his life there once was a little bit of Jesus in it," she chortled, offering me an out. "With you here, it's settled. We're doing Christmas. We'll make it a party. Do you want to invite your friend, what's-her-name? The person you came to see?"

"Rosemarie," I said. "And that's very generous of you."

"Well, you did come to Paris mostly to see her, didn't you?" Danielle asked. I didn't answer. I wasn't really sure anymore why I had come. "The phone is in your room," Danielle persisted. "Call. See if she's free. I think you said she's also on her own for Christmas?"

But when I did call, Rosemarie sounded exasperated about the invitation to dinner. "I'm so bored with Christmas," she said with a dramatic sigh. She was trying to sound archly witty, faking a New England accent to make her sound Katharine Hepburn—esque. "I was thinking to stay in, read Proust, ignore it. But." I heard her yawn through the phone. "My parents haven't sent me my money yet, and so I might be in the mood to eat. I mean, the larder is bare. Your friend, what's her name? She won't mind? And what does she do? Could she find me a job?" Concluding that the evening might benefit her in some way, Rosemarie agreed to arrive at Danielle's apartment at eight o'clock on Christmas Eve. "I think there's a bottle of champagne lying about somewhere," she said before hanging up, giving me the faintest hope that we might have a festive time after all. "I'll see if I can root it out from under the chaise."

Danielle was up early the next morning. I found her at her dining room table, writing out the next day's grocery list. Max had already gone out to jog in the park. "Husbands," Danielle said, crinkling her button nose. She had lived in France so long that she found the North American habit of sweating in public *dégoûtant,* disgusting. I still worked out, I told her, but in the privacy of a gym.

"I just walk everywhere," said Danielle smugly. "But I have to tell you," she continued, giggling. "Since Max, I've dropped a couple of sizes. Effortlessly, if you know what I mean." She'd never discussed sex with me, and I didn't really want to get into it then. I reached for the pot of coffee on the stove. "How about you?" she said. "Seeing anyone?"

"Nope," I said, hiding my face in my cup.

"Well, you're not getting any younger," she said.

I had come to Paris to be distracted. I had plans to go to the museums, shop, even interview someone famous for an article I would write up on my return. I wanted to keep up the illusion of a fabulous jet-set career. There was no room in my day timer for introspection. I told Danielle that I needed to get ready. But alone in my bedroom heaped with shiny new clothes, I wondered if I'd ever feel whole. I dressed with a mind to hiding all my flaws, pulling on black stockings and a dainty day suit with ruffles at the wrists. I was pretending. Playing someone I was not. A fraud.

I went back out to face Danielle. I asked if she thought I should wear the black shoes or the red.

"The black," said Danielle. "The red ones make you look like you're trying too hard."

I ARRIVED EARLY at Le Voltaire, a well-known bistro on the banks of the Seine, facing the Louvre. It was fifteen minutes to the hour, and no one was yet in the restaurant, or so I thought. When the maître d' approached, I said I had a rendezvous for lunch. *"Avec Monsieur Noureev?"* he asked. *Noureev* is how the French say the name of the great dancer Rudolf Nureyev. *"Oui,"* I said. He was the one I was to have lunch with that day, as part of a prearranged interview to promote an upcoming appearance Nureyev would be making in Toronto late the following month. It would be one of the last articles I would write for *The Globe and Mail* for five years. My swan song. But I didn't know that when I followed the maître d' to the back of the restaurant, where Nureyev was already sitting on a banquette, his back against a wall.

There, his sinewy neck wrapped round with the vibrant zigzag design of a Missoni scarf, his broad shoulders cloaked in tasselled shawls, his body erect, his nostrils flaring, his cheekbones a windswept plane, Nureyev sat like an oriental potentate, forbidding and proud.

He was reading. When I got close to the table I could see it was a heavily annotated musical score, a toccata by Bach. Nureyev folded the score away when he saw me approach. He didn't rise, but eyed me critically. I had the feeling that I stood too tall, that I ought to curtsy, something to honor his exalted presence.

The score, I could see, was worn from where he had been tracing the notes with his fingers, as if willing the baroque-era music to come alive at his touch. An idiosyncratic script crowded the margins. It was part Russian, part English, and augmented by nonverbal symbols borrowed from a system of dance notation known as choreology. More circles, spirals, and other signifiers of movement decorated spaces between octaves. Soon after I sat down in front of him, Nureyev said he was studying the score in hopes of becoming good enough to conduct the Bach piece for an audience. "An audience of friends," he hastened to add. "Who else would be polite enough to listen?" Nureyev's way of drawing out his vowels made you feel as if he was speaking in slow motion, as if each sentence might fill the long hours of a Russian White Night. I already had my pen and notebook out, recording everything he said. And he was saying he was getting ready to leave dance and reinvent himself as a conductor.

It was a stunning admission. Until then Nureyev had been defiant about not quitting dance before he, and he alone, felt ready. He was then fifty-three, well beyond the age when most dancers can still hope to perform. His landings had lately grown soft and wobbly. His once-powerful legs sometimes buckled under him from the strain. He was a ghost of what he once was, a dancer who since his defection to the West in 1963 had been universally celebrated for his magnetism and sensuality, second only to Vaslav Nijinsky. A story was circulating at that time concerning a woman in London who sued after seeing Nureyev in one of his recent performances, claiming that the dancer's decline had so shocked her senses that she became ill.

I asked him why he had persisted. The question was relevant to my story. After all, he was supposed to be dancing again in just over a month's time, and before a paying audience. But I wasn't sure how he'd react; his temper was legendary. Incidents in which he slapped his partners were widely reported. The Russian ballerina Natalia Makarova once accused him of deliberately dropping her on the stage in Paris. I felt the flash of his green eyes penetrate my soul, but then he answered without further hesitation. "You have talent, and it dictates your life," he said with a Tartar shrug. "It possesses. It's what people want to see in theater. People obsessed by what they do."

He leaned his body across the table, coming within inches of my face. "You like Giselle," he pronounced, referring to the title character in the French ballet, who dies of a broken heart. "That good," he said, banging a hand on the table. I didn't know what he meant and didn't ask him to explain. I was hoping he was referring to the ballet's white-on-white ending, when Giselle comes back to life, resurrected by love as symbolized by a neverending ghostly dance.

We continued talking about dance, the classics, the difference between dancers today and dancers in the past. Our conversation veered in the direction of the Opéra de Paris, the original, not the Bastille. Nureyev had lately been artistic director of the Paris Opera Ballet there. His autocratic management style had brought him into conflict with the executive director, Pierre Bergé. At that time, Nureyev had been demoted to the position of artist in residence. We all have our workplace challenges I thought to myself. Nureyev described the ballet he had recently staged for the company, a production of *Don Quixote* that would be performed at the Palais Garnier the day after Christmas. He asked me if I was planning on going. I wasn't, but instead of saying that, I told him I had never seen a ballet at the Palais Garnier. It was my turn to make the stunning admission. Nureyev looked at me as if I had just said I'd never been kissed.

"You come to ballet. Now! I take you. Come!" His eyes blazed, not at me, but at our hovering waiter who scurried over with the bill.

As Nureyev was my guest, I would pay the tab—or rather, my newspaper would. The amount was almost a thousand French francs, a princely sum for a meal that had consisted of deliberately undercooked lamb—bloody meat for the tiger, tiger, burning bright before me—and raw vegetables.

I fumbled for my credit card. To my horror, it was rejected. Not this time for lack of funds. *"On n'accepte pas les cartes,"* the waiter said. I had forgotten that the credit card, whose status is ubiquitous on my side of the Atlantic, has little or no value in Paris. Restaurants commonly reject plastic in favor of cash or checks. But I had no cash to speak of. I was as good as dead.

Nureyev leaned back into the banquette, looking very much like Prince Siegfried in *Swan Lake* when he is forced to wait out the coquettish dances of the princesses all vying for his hand in marriage. He raised an eyebrow.

I saw myself washing the dishes in the back room, the sleeves of my faux-Chanel suit rolled up over the elbows. I thought of Nureyev slapping me, kicking the furniture on his way out. I saw the gendarmes. I wondered if the Canadian embassy took on sad cases like mine.

"I can't pay the bill," I finally admitted.

Nureyev regarded me in silence. "I pay. You pay back." He slapped his book of personal checks on the table. In France they are as big as lamb chops. They were linen-colored with his name, address, and phone number in black cursive letters in the far upper-right-hand corner. He pushed them my way. "Write. Go."

I opened his checkbook carefully, as if it were the *Book of Hours,* Nureyev nodding his head in encouragement. I wrote out the day's date, the sum, and the name of the receiver of Nureyev's money, Le Voltaire. I stopped at the blank space where his signature would go. I looked at him questioningly. He thrust his chin out at me, nudging me to hurry along, finish the task.

I inhaled deeply and, steadying my hand, I wrote in letters appropriately large and stately the exalted name "Rudolf Nureyev" as if it were my own. I was now guilty of impersonating a famous Russian dancer, truly culpable of fraud.

He was pleased. He explained that he didn't want cash as payback. He wanted the equivalent in smoked salmon, which he said he would have for Christmas. He would be spending the day with the Rothschilds, he said. I assumed he meant the salmon would be for them. He told me that I would go to Fauchon to get it. This was the stupendously expensive *épicerie* near the Madeleine, where fur-wrapped patrons didn't bat an eye when buying $35 pots of jam.

"But first we go." He grabbed my hand, commanding, "*Vas-y!*"

I didn't question. I didn't want to let go. I let him run me out the door and toward gallery-laden Rue du Bac, the street I used to walk en route to the Louvre when I lived as a babysitter on Rue de l'Université, just steps from where we then were standing.

He hurried. The number 68 bus was at that moment slamming to a stop at the corner. Still holding my hand, Nureyev jumped inside first, executing a facsimile of the gravity-defying leaps he had performed on the world stage. I, by necessity, leapt after him—the nymph following the faun. He threw a fistful of change into the box and led me to the back. There were no vacant seats, so we were forced to stand. Nureyev put my hand on the chrome pole to steady my balance on the bumpy ride taking us across the bridge over the Seine. He held on tightly himself and turned to face me. We were standing chest to chest, eye to eye.

Standing, I could see how short he was. On stage he looked like a giant. That is true of most dancers. They have the ability to lengthen their limbs, their torsos, their necks, to appear larger than life, superhuman, as if unfettered by physical limitations. Inwardly I pinched myself and told myself not to blink, not to miss a second, never to forget.

It was one thing to interview a celebrity, quite another to be pulled into the everyday life of one. I felt I had become part of the Nureyev story. He had been born on a moving train. I was now with him on a moving bus, rocking back and forth into his body, locked in a pedestrian pas de deux. I held my breath. I had become tied to a star.

Everyone on the bus did a double take. I imagined it was like suddenly noticing a Beatle in your midst. People stared, gasped, looked away, stared again, not knowing what to do or say. Nureyev ignored it all, imperiously. He was standing in ballet's widely spaced second position to keep from rolling with the rollicking momentum of the bus. Forbidding and proud.

Just when it seemed that I would burst from holding my breath, Nureyev, without warning, suddenly grabbed my hand again and pushed me out the back door onto the street. Cars whizzed by; bodies jostled for space on the sidewalk. I was temporarily lost, and then Nureyev turned me around to face Mecca.

We were on the Place de l'Opéra, just outside the Palais Garnier, home of the Paris Opera Ballet. One of the world's largest theaters, it rose from the square in a swirl of rose-colored marble columns and sculptured friezes. It looked like a wedding cake, elaborately decorated with an enormous sweeping staircase out front and topped by an undulating roof weathered to a beautiful green patina. A gilded statue was on the roof. It depicted Apollo, god of music, holding his lyre to the heavens. Nureyev had paused for a moment to let me fill my eyes. Taking hold of my hand again, he said, "Come!" and pulled me deeper into his world.

He led me solicitously through the swirl of Paris traffic encircling the theater, never once letting go of me. He held my hand as a father might do, proudly leading me to his place of work, showing it off to me and me to it. He was smiling and walking at a quick clip. His feet were turned out in that splayed position shared by all ballet dancers as a result of having distorted their skeletons at a young age in service of their art. Which is to say, he walked like a duck.

He led me toward the back, through the stage-door entrance, which led to a slow decline from the street, a downward walk into the bowels of the theater. The cavernous passageway had low ceilings and perspiring stone walls. The lighting was scant, and as our footsteps echoed down the tunnel-like corridor, I saw our lengthening shadows darkening the pathway before us.

I didn't know where we were going but I mutely followed along, trusting him emphatically. With each step I became aware of others who had walked there before me, all the great dancers and choreographers and set designers and composers and musicians and impresarios and directors and patrons and writers and seamstresses and scenery painters and broom pushers and secretaries and patrons and groupies—anyone great or small with some connection, major or minor, with Paris and its wondrous world of art.

Nureyev turned me left and right through this backstage maze. Along the way we encountered a cleaning woman, her head wrapped in a kerchief, and an elevator operator who took us up and up and up. The backstage of the Palais Garnier is so deep it is said to harbor a subterranean lake. Nureyev squeezed my hand. He must have known he was giving me the thrill of a lifetime, and he seemed to be enjoying the moment every bit as much as I was.

We emerged from the darkness toward a shaft of light. We were suddenly in the wings. He looked at me, grinning. He put a finger to his lips, urging me to be quiet. Some of the Paris Opera dancers were rehearsing, and he wanted to watch them unawares.

In the pit, members of the orchestra tuned their instruments. Three dancers, dressed in sweats and heavy socks, a Degas-like vision of the toil and tedium behind the glamor of theater life, fell into position on the steeply raked stage. A ballet mistress barked out their counts. The music played.

Together, the trio rose on *demi-pointe*, extending their back legs into an arabesque. Collectively they turned, locking hands to perform a *pas de trois*, a lyrical dance for three. They stumbled over a tricky section of choreography requiring them to end their series of turns with a forward thrust of a pointed foot. One arm was simultaneously to go onto the hip while the other swept outward in a gesture of welcome. With each stumble, the ballet mistress loudly clapped her hands for the music to stop, making the dancers take their positions from the top. I could see their beautifully squared shoulders slump from frustration. The moment reminded me that ballet is an art that constantly reproves the dancer, making her feel rarely good enough. Dancers have told me that no matter how spectacularly they may have performed for an audience the night before, the next morning there was always a daily class where the ballet coach would, despite the fatigue and sore muscles, make them go through their paces again, one step at a time. The stay at the top of the mountain was never long.

Nureyev watched his put-upon babies with an arm wrapped around his barrel-like chest. He also held one hand to his face to hide a devilish smile that was growing there. The sequence the dancers were trying to perform was hard. He knew, because he had created it. It was his *Don Quixote,* the ballet about the man who chases dreams in the form of windmills. He seemed to relish their struggle, like a parent watching a child stumble in taking its first steps. At lunch he had told me he was proud of the Paris dancers. He called them his artists. I had the impression that he allowed them their mistakes on the road to perfection, if only to encourage them to be better.

But he had seen enough. Pushing me gently aside and, without saying a word, but right on the music, Nureyev burst from his hiding place in the wings. Just like that, he executed three flawless turns, thrust his leg forward, as if saying ta-dah! with his body. He brought his hand sharply to his waist, making a sweeping gesture that, when he did it, no longer looked like a polite hello. It was more a bugle call, a signal to look his way, drop everything, and salute!

The dancers squealed with delight. They loved the surprise of him, the impishness of him waiting silently behind the curtains before making an impromptu entrance, upstaging them all. It was instantly clear that he was still the gold standard. The idea was to imitate him. The mere presence of him got the dancers excitedly moving again. They hurried to take their places. They mimicked his steps and, above all, his supreme self-confidence. Despite his advanced years, Nureyev was still capable of working magic, of transforming the dancers into superdynamos, of galvanizing everyone around him merely with an artful kick of the leg.

Nureyev looked to me to see how I was enjoying his impromptu performance. I was delighted, of course, and as I made eye contact, I smiled broadly at him, and he at me. I stayed a while longer in the wings, watching him instruct the dancers. He had them laughing. The image was poignant. The great dancer, in his street clothes, signs of age traced on his face, was imparting to the next generation what he knew. He was passing the torch. I was aware that such greatness might never come our way again. I left to go buy the salmon, returning later to leave $200 worth of beautifully wrapped fish with the theater's backstage concierge.

WHEN I AWOKE on Christmas Eve, Danielle had already set the table. On top of a saffron-yellow tablecloth she had laid out three large pink dinner plates and an oversized, handcrafted green-and-purple ceramic candlestick that looked like an eggplant, another well-intentioned wedding gift, no doubt.

"I've always liked the look of Christmas, the lights and color," she said. She then brandished a list, which was sizeable. She said we had many ingredients to buy because in Paris, Christmas Eve had its own special meal, and we were going to follow the tradition as if we had both been born into it.

We walked together outside her apartment. The air was damp and cold. Danielle, her heels clicking rapidly on the sidewalk, me tagging along, explained what was on the agenda. A goose. And that goose, she instructed, speaking loudly as we squeezed past the surging crowds on the constricted sidewalks of her centuries-old neighborhood, needed to be accompanied by a *boudin blanc*—a white blood sausage. And that had to come with wine-soaked shredded cabbage and roasted chestnuts and, for dessert, an ooze of brie and something sugary called a *bûche*.

To get all these ingredients, we needed to go to a half-dozen different small shops, each with a different name—*boulangerie, épicerie, charcuterie, fromagerie, pâtisserie*. I had rarely experienced the domestic side of Paris before, having usually been an itinerant tourist without a kitchen, and I was enjoying the view, even if it did occasionally involve whole heads of goat in some of the storefront windows.

We walked down the Rue du Faubourg Saint-Antoine, where we had at our disposal a number of small specialty shops selling coffee and snails and chairs and mirrors. The area was once the furniture-making center of Paris and still bore the imprint of generations of wood workers who had come before. I breathed in the air, dreaming of sawdust and other smells associated with an industrious class of people. But my senses were occluded by the tang of fresh-baked bread. Danielle had navigated across the street, to a bakery near the corner of Rue Daval and Rue de la Roquette. She said it was famous for its *pain lyonnais*, a hearty loaf made of whole grains, a bread made for the workers.

It was crowded inside, and Danielle stood in line. The croissants, I could determine from a collective clucking of tongues, were already sold out. I took the chance to study the antiquated interior. On the walls were frescoes of maidens in idyllic fields, gathering their wheat. Gold-colored moldings shaped like spring garlands framed each image. More paintings decorated the ceiling, at the center of which was a portrait of Demeter, goddess of the grain. Danielle elbowed me from behind. "Get going," she said, as more people pushed inside the bakery's doors. "You're kind of in the way."

Outside, where the winter sky was bruised black and blue, Danielle offered me a bite from a *ficelle,* a loaf even skinnier than a baguette, about the width of two fingers. "I noticed you didn't eat breakfast," she said. "That's why you're acting so dazed."

The bread was hot and moist, straight from the oven. "Worth the wait, huh?" Danielle said, her cheeks flushed and full.

The extravagant visual presentation in the food shops rivalled the Louvre. As we scurried down the Rue de Lappe, I saw store windows full of holiday meats, all beautifully displayed. I paused to marvel at guinea fowl so artistically trussed with filigrees of fat and prune and colored vegetable that they looked more like Fabergé eggs than carcasses. Danielle had seen it all before and, when she went inside, she simply asked for one of the pretty little pot roasts to be wrapped up in brown paper. I watched, spellbound. This wasn't a visit to the butcher's as I knew it: this was a boutique for carnivores.

Danielle was hurrying now, racing against the watery sun. As I tried to keep pace with her, I didn't mind my way. I stepped in dog poop and skidded. I collided with a woman holding a full-to-bursting shopping bag. She glowered, even as I tried to apologize. *"Américaine!"* I heard her mutter as she trudged away.

Danielle had kept on walking. "I'll have to have a bath when we get back to the apartment," I said when I caught up to her. The wet tobacco—colored turd under my foot smelled violently sour. I stopped to scrape my sole against a curb, but was almost hit by someone trying to park. A horn blared loudly.

"I'm concerned about you," said Danielle. "You have no sense of time. You just do what you want, when you want, talk without thinking. You're out of control."

Her words wounded.

We continued in silence. I had fallen into a sulk. "I'm just trying to be your friend, you know," Danielle finally said as we trudged with the parcels up the five flights of curving stairs. Several times, the hallways plunged into darkness after the timer on the light switch had run its course. Danielle fumbled in the dark to push buttons on the various floors to allow us to see our way.

Inside the apartment Max had erected a tree. As lean as Danielle was fleshy, Max squinted up at us from behind gold-wire glasses, asking us heartily if we'd had a good time. Danielle dropped her bundles in the kitchen and went over to kiss him, with a *hmmm* sound, on his pale, puckered lips. He was on his knees in a corner of the living room. He had found a spot just big enough to accommodate the dwarfish evergreen, and was just then stringing it with lights.

He looked at Danielle, then at me, then at Danielle.

"Everything okay?" he asked.

Danielle shot him a narrow-eyed look that said, we'll talk about it later. Married only months, and already they had a shorthand. I told Danielle I needed a peeler for the potatoes and retreated to the kitchen.

I worked quickly and quietly. I cut the tops off the green beans. I washed the lettuce. Danielle put the meat in the oven. We were civil with each other, saying please and thank-you and excuse me as we worked like two chefs in a very small kitchen, an efficient cooking team, to get the grandiose meal ready in time. When I announced that I really had to take that bath—I needed to wash away the day's worries—Danielle shrugged and said, "Go ahead then."

The doorbell rang. I was wrapped in a towel in my makeshift room. I reached for a dress and chose the emerald-green satin, thinking it right for the occasion. I poked a wet head of hair out my door to ask Danielle to fasten me. "You're incorrigible," Danielle said to me as she zipped me quickly. "But anyway, Merry Christmas," she said. "Merry Christmas," I replied, as together we opened the door to a beribboned bottle of champagne.

Rosemarie and I embraced. I introduced her to Danielle and Max. They all embraced each other in turn, acting very cosmopolitan, very French. Rosemarie had dressed up for the party in a sparkling blouse and shoulder-length earrings. I told her she looked nice. "Nice dress," she said to me after sitting down on a chair in the living room. The edges of her mouth rode up and down, her eyes darted left and right, just like a puppet's. "You look like one of those Christmas presents you get wrapped at the mall for free."

Her comment made Danielle laugh. Max laughed, too. I smiled and offered to pour the champagne.

Rosemarie's long and naturally wavy hair was already streaked with silver, despite her being just thirty-four years old. When she talked she played with it, wrapping it around her fingers and piling it on top of her head before letting it drop over one shoulder and then the other. She asked Max how long they had had the apartment, how much they paid for it, did they know of any places in the neighborhood coming up for rent. She said she liked the location. Max told her about the renovation. Rosemarie touched his knee and nodded. Danielle and I went into the kitchen to begin bringing out the evening's various courses.

I ladled the oxtail soup, on top of which Danielle had sprinkled freshly chopped parsley, and thought, I won't last the evening.

Rosemarie had now tied her hair to the back of her head in a loose knot, tendrils falling at the side of each ear. She flirted with everyone at the table. Her liveliness was what prevented the party from becoming an utter disaster. Danielle always had a soft spot for eccentrics, and she seemed to like Rosemarie. That night she laughed at Rosemarie's naughty jokes and encouraged her to tell of her Paris adventures at Willi's, an American wine bar near the Bourse where she worked part-time as a waitress. Max leaned in as Rosemarie described the so-called expats, financiers like him, in their suits and ties. The literary scene had long ago decamped for New York. "To hear them talk," Rosemarie said, tucking into the white blood sausage that squirted transparent juices and a fragrant smell of fennel, "Money is the new poetry. Seeing how expensive it is to live in Paris, I think they're right."

Max said more money could easily be made in the States. "But I'm in Paris because you can't put a price on beauty, and Paris is one beautiful town."

I went to the kitchen to get the red-wine cabbage, glad to leave the table. We were a small group, strangers really, celebrating Christmas in a city not our own, eating food we didn't normally eat, far away from our own families, pretending, each of us, that we were having a marvellous time.

I brought out the goose that before going into the oven had been dressed like a courtier, with sliced olives as buttons down its puffed-out chest and red pepper as trim. The color had burned away in the oven, and it was now just a regulation Christmas goose. Still, it cut a dashing figure when placed on the table. When I sliced into it, steam rising from the incision, Max and Rosemarie raised a glass to Danielle and me. We had actually pulled it off, a real French dinner.

As we were eating our *bûche*, a chocolaty confection resembling a Christmas log, Danielle broached the topic of the nativity. "Like most Jews," she said, "I've never understood how you Christians can buy into this idea of an immaculate conception. I mean, that's the biggest cuck-olding story around, right?"

Rosemarie laughed. Her family had been Catholic, but she hadn't been to church in years. "I can think of better things to do while sitting on the floor on my knees," she said saucily.

Max blushed.

"I was an illegitimate birth," I blurted. I had finished the champagne and was into my third glass of wine.

The table went silent.

"My mother said she got pregnant with me on purpose. She wanted someone to love her."

"What a bunch of bullshit," said Rosemarie.

"I don't think so," I said, taken aback. "It means she wanted me."

Rosemarie rolled her eyes. She didn't know of my work troubles, had never met my mother, didn't know I was feeling vulnerable. "That's a lot of pressure to put on a kid, don't you think? Jeez, and I thought my Polack mother was a piece of work."

"Yes, I think my friend here is more Jewish than I am," quipped Danielle. "She's a sucker for guilt." Danielle winked at me. I smiled faintly back.

"I know!" I suddenly shouted. The others looked at me, startled. "I propose midnight mass at Notre Dame."

"That would just give me the creeps," replied Danielle.

"Sorry," Max said. "I haven't been to mass in years."

"I'm not saying you have to go to confession," I said. "Let's just go. All of us. Come on. It's a Paris tradition. We'll light a candle."

All eyes landed on Rosemarie.

"Please," I said. I no longer cared if it sounded like begging. Danielle left the room, but soon reappeared with a cache of gifts.

"Speaking of Paris traditions," she said. "I did some research and found out that on Christmas Eve, you are supposed to give gifts."

I gasped. I hadn't bought her anything.

Danielle put a wrapped parcel in front of me. Inside was a strangely shaped backpack, narrow at the top, wide at the bottom. It looked like it was made to carry a violin. "It's the Eiffel Tower," said Danielle, grinning. "I hope you like it." She was a kind soul, and at that moment I was sorry we had fought. For Rosemarie she had bought a ballpoint pen with a pink feather at the top. "I heard you like to write."

"Now get thee to a nunnery," she scolded. "Leave me and my husband alone."

Rosemarie stood up from the table. The gift giving had turned her suddenly charitable. She reluctantly agreed to join me on my journey to Notre Dame. "But I'm warning you," she said. "The crowds will be awful."

I WOKE LATE on Christmas Day, past noon, to find myself alone in Danielle's apartment. She and Max had left early in the morning to catch their flight to the Bahamas. She had left me a note on the table, which still bore signs of the party from the night before, saying good-bye. I wandered from room to room, not sure what to do with myself. I watched French television. I tried to read a book, but couldn't concentrate. I browsed through a pile of old newspapers. I made café au lait, and put on some music. I looked out the window at all the other windows closing in on the apartment and saw the old man across the way. He was looking out his window. He caught me looking at him and, in a huff, slammed his shutters closed. I reached for the telephone. I had one number in Paris, the number belonging to a stranger, but a famous stranger. I dialled it—I had nothing to lose, I thought.

"Yes!"

Nureyev himself answered the phone with a terrifying monosyllable, tossed like a grenade, as if the ringing had been a great nuisance to him.

I reminded him who I was, the Canadian who had been with him three days earlier.

"Yes! Yes!" he said again, impatient.

"Why you not wait?"

"Pardon?"

"Why you not wait at Opéra? To eat with me. Eat salmon. Come to my apartment!"

I felt the blood drain from my face. I hadn't realized his intentions.

"Well, um, sorry, I didn't know," I said. "So, um, you got it then, the salmon?"

"Yes. Divine. Too bad you not wait. But you come again. To Opéra. *Don Quixote*. You come backstage, after. Come see me!"

Nureyev abruptly hung up, and for a long while I sat there, holding my end of the phone, stupefied by his suggestion that I was to have had dinner with him. I couldn't believe that I had misunderstood and lost what would have been a once-in-a-lifetime opportunity to have dined with Nureyev, *chez lui*.

I reflected again on the rarity of him as I dressed the following night to go to the ballet. The evening's performers were Nureyev's protégés, the long-limbed Sylvie Guillem and the dashing Patrick Dupond, rival to the throne at the Paris Opera and, indeed, its then-new artistic director. They constituted ballet royalty. I inwardly thrilled at the mere mention of their names. I took a taxi to the theater and entered through the front doors this time. Where backstage was a dark labyrinth housing mysteries, front of house was bright, expansive, and palatial. Everything was so luxurious, it could have been Versailles. Outside Paris was gloomy, but there, at the ballet, it was eternal summer I thought as I admired the mosaic ceiling, the golden chandeliers, the walls of gilt-edged mirrors. I climbed the grand staircase made of marble, already feeling uplifted. I handed a uniformed usher my ticket and was shown to my seat. And not just any seat. Nureyev had put me in the box reserved for dignitaries. It was front and center, where a person of great distinction was supposed to sit. I couldn't believe my good fortune. But more, I couldn't get over Nureyev's generosity, his desire to please encompassing every detail and extending to me, someone relatively unfamiliar to him.

The curtain rose on a performance that, from start to finish, was a blistering, fast-paced romp through Cervantes' castanets-clacking Spain. It was raucous, robust, a pyrotechnic showcase for the unsurpassed talents of the Paris Opera dancers. I sat on the edge of my seat throughout, thrilled to have been a part of it, each step, each twirl, each jump and unshakeable balance forever seared on my memory.

When the last of the ballet's three acts was over, I rushed backstage, eager to see Nureyev again and to thank him for making my first experience of the Paris ballet so extraordinary and wonderful. He was there, waiting for me. Initially I had breezed right past him; I had hardly recognized him. He seemed oddly diminished in comparison to the magnificence of the evening. His clothes hung loosely on his withered frame. They looked slept in. Their drabness accentuated the forlornness of his solitary figure. I felt sad to see him like this. He was the artist whose trailblazing dancing had set the standard for the young dancers who had impressed us that night with their iron-clad technique, their sparkling presence. They were, like all the dancers who have come after him and benefited from his gifts, Nureyev's disciples. He watched them from the sidelines, as if tacitly acknowledging his glory days to be over.

I approached, and when he saw me, he flashed me a ready smile. "Not bad, huh?" He winked at me, and leading me by the elbow, took me over to meet his principal dancers. He called them *mes enfants*.

I was aware of the background story. Relations between him and Guillem were reportedly stormy. She had lately announced her decision to leave Paris for the Royal Ballet in London. Dupond, meanwhile, was being portrayed in press reports as the usurper of Nureyev's throne. The mercurial Pierre Bergé had recently appointed him artistic director of the Paris Opera after demoting Nureyev to artist in residence. That was the gossip, and the journalist in me wanted to see how things would play out. Would there be a scene? Would I have a scoop? Yet when the two principal dancers saw Nureyev walking in their direction, they shook off the backstage admirers asking for their autographs and focused all their attention anxiously on him. They were like schoolchildren waiting for the verdict— pass or fail. Both still had on their costumes and were in full makeup. Perspiration had dampened their eager-looking faces. I stood aside to watch as Nureyev took each by the hand. Looking them in the eyes, he told them they had made him proud. *"Je suis très fier,"* he said. *"Très fier."* Both dancers emitted loud exhalations of relief. Guillem leaned toward him to lay her head on his chest. Her tiara got caught on his scarf. He untangled her, and then she limped away, eager, I thought, to get out of her pointe shoes.

The dancers had done their job: they had satisfied him. That was all that mattered. They were free to go to their dressing rooms and wash away the face paint, become mere mortals again.

I turned to look at the former god of the dance standing before me. He was also a mere mortal, flawed like the rest of us. We were soon sandwiched between sycophants and other hangers-on as fans started to crowd him. I said my good-byes. I mentioned that I would be at his upcoming performance in Toronto, but even as I said it, I knew there was no chance for a repeat encounter. This had been a rare occasion. It had been like ballet itself—beautiful, but gone in an instant.

When I got back to Danielle's empty apartment, I was still high with excitement. I had no one to tell my story to, so I wrote a postcard to my mother. I quoted Théophile Gautier, a pioneer of dance criticism and a Parisian, who had written on the rise of the Romantic ballet: "All things turn to dust/Save beauty fashioned well." I hoped that my mother would understand me. Ballet was my tree house in the wilderness, where no one else in my family went save me. It was an art form known for escapism, but it brought me face to face with myself. My dreams.

I looked out the window, Paris twinkling in the darkness. In that moment I was aware of myself as being one of the millions of stars in the universe that together create the light by which we can see the heavens. I was part of the constellation called humanity. I thought of my newspaper, the reason I had come to Paris, the reason I had connected with Nureyev. "Please God, don't let me lose my job." The words popped out of me before I even knew what I was doing. "I will go back to Toronto. I will eat crow. I will submit. Please, I love writing. I love art. Don't take them away from me."

I had finally said the prayer that had gotten stuck in my throat at the tourist parade that had been Notre Dame. I fell asleep, fully clothed, on top of the upstairs marital bed.

LIFE ISN'T A ballet. In reality, the curtain doesn't fall on a tidy ending. I did return to Toronto. I did try to be humble. I found a skating show to review, something I thought I could tackle with some competence, thinking it to be dance on ice.

The leads were Katarina Witt and Brian Boitano, she from Germany, he from the United States. My thesis was that by pushing the limits of their own sport, these dynamos on blades were transporting skating out of the arena and into the world of art. An editor with knowledge of figure skating looked over my shoulder. I had asked him for advice. I hadn't wanted to make any mistakes.

In the final minutes before the deadline, he suggested I Canadianize the content. "Isn't Kurt Browning now at the top of his game?" he asked me. "He is famous for something. What is it?" I had at my disposal the skating show press kit, and I quickly opened it. People were screaming for my copy. I flipped rapidly through the pages. Aha! There it was: "A quadruple toe-loop completed three-quarters of a second before landing." Browning had just performed the maneuver at the Winter Olympics. I showed the phrase to the editor. "That it?" I asked. "That's it," he said.

With seconds to go before deadline, I typed the phrase into my story. I copied it verbatim, and deliberately so. I thought it was an accurate description of what had made Browning special. The article was edited and published, and that seemed to be the end of that.

But a few days later, a letter of complaint arrived at the paper. The writer said in his letter that I had "parroted" an expression that had originally appeared in a magazine article on Browning. Included in my press kit, it was what I had relied on to nail the technical description. It ended up nailing me. Siding with this letter-writer 100 percent, management seized on the article as evidence that I was a plagiarist, tried and true. I had not learned my lesson. On February 15, 1991, I was fired. A security guard escorted me to my desk. I was ordered to pack up my things and immediately leave the building.

The assumption was that I would never return, but I knew I had done nothing wrong. I had to fight back. I launched a grievance, backed by the newspaper's union. It was while fighting for my reputation—really, my life— that I experienced a sea change. I grew from being fixated on the outside of me to caring for the inside. I grew to value kindness above all other human traits. It was part of learning to be kind to myself. For a long time I had hated myself, and that self-loathing continued for the first few years following my expulsion. As soon as I lost my job, I cut off all my long hair. I thought often of killing myself. I stopped going to the theater. I stopped going out.

I contemplated abandoning writing altogether and eventually went back to university, the only place where I had previously felt blameless, where I had succeeded on my own merits. I contemplated a life as a scholar in the remote field of Medieval Studies. Where that idea came from, I still don't know.

But ultimately I came around to the fact that I was a writer. It was what I did. It was what I wanted to do and, more importantly, needed to do. Writing was my identity.

In the final year of my litigation battle, writing assignments from other magazines and newspapers started trickling my way, after the stink of being accused of plagiarism had left me blackballed from my own industry for a very long time. One editor at a rival newspaper told me that he had been "warned" off me by people at the *Globe*, but then relented after listening to my side of the story. Another, employed at a different publication, reported to me that she too had been told by members of *Globe* management to stay clear of me. "But I made up my own mind when I saw how long and hard you were fighting," she said. "I thought, she must not be guilty as they say she is, at all." I was back writing, but not especially because some of these people still considered me good at it, but more because they were kind and willing to form their own opinions about me, instead of following, like sheep, the status quo. To them I was David battling the Goliath of all Canadian newspapers. Said one, "I want to publish you in my pages because politically, journalistically, it feels the right thing to do." These odd-job writing assignments didn't end up paying much, but it didn't matter. I had streamlined my life. I had moved to a low-rent apartment and learned to cook modest meals. I was, in my small, day-by-day way, learning how to be content with not very much at all.

Nureyev had called me "Giselle." But in those days I felt more like Cinderella, happy as long as I was quietly toiling away. For a long time he remained my secret. I told no one, least of all my mother, what the legendary dancer had done for me. I didn't want her to spoil the magic of that time in Paris with some flippant remark about how I needed to stop, once and for all, mooning over the ballet.

She had never understood what she called my "obsession."

Nureyev died of AIDS on January 6, 1993, almost exactly two years after my cherished encounter with him. I watched his funeral on a scratchy television in my new, threadbare Toronto digs. He lay in state in the very place to which he had once taken me, hand in hand.

As I watched the international dignitaries streaming past his body, I recalled how Nureyev had put me in a seat reserved for luminaries, how he had granted me a rare glimpse into his world of hard work and beauty. I remembered also the warmth and strength of his hand as he led me through Paris in search of a mutually cherished dream— the transcendent power of art. I cried for the loss of him, the loss of my dream.

But, and I guess this is the happily ever after part, I won. I got my job back, my reputation restored. A thirteen-word technical term describing a skating maneuver did not constitute plagiarism, an arbitrator ruled in a precedent-setting, sixty-eight-page judgment. As for the merits of the previous charge, the article involving arts medicine used by management to establish a pattern of behavior, it was considered so weak that it was thrown out of court.

I was, to my surprise, awarded almost four years of back pay, then equivalent to the cost of a decent downtown Toronto house. The *Globe* had early on offered me a small cash settlement, likely hoping I would go away quietly. But I wasn't fighting for the money. All I had ever wanted was what I prayed for that night in Paris—my job and, through it, my connection to the world of art left intact.

This was a huge win, a trailblazing case that made national headlines. But the accusations had turned some colleagues against me, perhaps because they were frightened that they could be next. There was one notable exception. One colleague had early on volunteered to assist in fighting the charge against me. He said that what I was being accused of, lifting a description of a fact from a press kit, was par for the course in daily journalism. "If this charge is allowed to stand," he had said, first in a passionate letter announcing his interest in defending me and later on the stand, "then all journalists stand on a gallows trapdoor." It is said that it takes just one good man in a room of a hundred to make a difference. He was my one good man.

But there was another accomplice: my mother. While she was, through most of my tear-stained battle, struggling with her own financial ups and downs, and was eventually forced to declare bankruptcy herself (like mother, like daughter), her advice to me to document events at work proved invaluable. My prodigious memory combined with my equally prodigious note-taking had the opposition so tongue-tied that at one point the company's counsel, trying to discredit me, accused me of having doctored my notes after the fact, inserting self-serving lies in them. To which I replied that it had been my mother who had advised me, my mother who had smelled the rat, my mother who had properly instructed me as to what to do. "And," I said, my voice rising with genuine feeling for the first time in the trial (I was meant to seem cool and unflustered, at a remove from the maelstrom raging around me), "my mother is always right!" As soon as I said it, I knew I would probably never live it down.

The evening of my win, though, the first call I made was to her. I was sobbing and hyperventilating as if I had just been told of the death of a loved one (and in a way it was a death: the death of the old me, the end of my life on trial, the demise of my sullied reputation). To celebrate the news, she spent the last money in her purse on a large bouquet of roses and a bottle of champagne, which we drank that night in my tiny apartment. I hadn't any champagne glasses, so we drank from coffee mugs.

I got through that long, cold, isolating period by reflecting often on Nureyev. His lesson to me was to have faith in deliverance. It had worked for him, leading him out of the darkness of Communism and into the brightness of the world's stage. He seemed instinctively to know that it would work for me, too. I took that as his undying gift to me, his power to restore in me the belief that the creative life is the route to self-liberty.

And so I had been right all along to believe that Paris would come to my rescue. "You have a talent and it dictates your life. It possesses . . ."

SIX

Fiancée

· 1995 ·

"The supreme happiness of life is the conviction
that we are loved."

VICTOR HUGO, *LES MISÉRABLES*

I RETURNED TO Paris five years later with the man I would
marry. Bringing him there just weeks after we were
engaged had been a test. I knew instinctively that I loved
him, but I still needed assurance that he was the One. In
Paris I was looking for proof that we were truly compatible.
Would he love the city as I loved it? Would he find in it a
manifestation of all his dreams, hopes, fears, and desires?
If so, I believed, we would live happily ever after.

The entire flight over, I had been apprehensive. But as soon as we arrived in Paris, after an eight-hour flight, I realized I needn't worry. Victor sat on the seat next to me inside an airport bus. We snuggled up close to each other the entire ride in, oblivious to the wall of standing passengers bumping along next to us. The windows were large as movie screens, and we delighted in what to us were unseasonably green fields rolling past us as we sped along the A1 motorway. As the fields turned into cement blocks, signalling our approach into the city, Victor craned his neck to see for the first time the massive bulge of Paris rising beguilingly from the banks of the Seine. The golden letters on café awnings seemed at once to catch his ever-widening eyes. I watched as he devoured the wrought-iron railings on second-floor balconies, the bright-hued advertisements adorning buildings with larger-than-life images of sultry women clasping bottles of amber perfume. He observed the corrugated metal covers on shop windows not yet open for the day, and an equine effigy overhanging one where horse meat was sold. Water from the street cleaners' parade at dawn still lay heavily on city streets, making them sparkle beneath the sun. I heard Victor say out loud Saint-Raphaël, the name of a local aperitif that he saw painted onto the side of an old brick building. And then he said "beautiful," declaring out loud that to him, at least, this riot of urban color and detail was a thing of art.

The bus had come to a stop near Place de la Concorde. The doors opened and we both leapt out, and then Victor started laughing. The sun was so bright he needed his sunglasses. Before he put them on, I could see his chocolate brown eyes wrinkling at the corners as he fought the glare. He slipped on his shades and, looking at me, smiled in wonder. His entire being radiated pleasure. "Feel that energy," he said, inhaling deeply, filling his lungs with this vision of Paris as life force. Horns blared and exhaust spewed as we bent to pick up our luggage, which the driver had hurled out from under the belly of the bus. Victor laughed some more. I started laughing with him, swept up by his unbridled enthusiasm. It was February. Toronto, which we had just left behind, was blanketed by winter, its skies low and putty-gray. But in Paris birds sang loudly from the branches of trees while daffodils, rising brilliantly from their frosty beds, danced freely with the wind. A pathetic fallacy, perhaps. But I can say for certain that Paris was resplendent on the day of my long-awaited return, and I shall never forget how in that instant I felt that I had done the right thing in coming back. My world was indeed beautiful again.

Victor held my hand as we hailed a taxi that first morning together in Paris. It was an uphill ride to Montmartre, and our tiny hotel was located next door to the Sacré-Cœur basilica. We would spend the next week perched high above Paris, lovers floating on clouds. The taxi pushed through streets so narrow I thought it would scrape up against the other cars tightly parked on both sides. We held on tight to each other as the driver advanced at a fevered speed. Victor leaned in to me and said how his older brother, who had come to Paris for his honeymoon fifteen years earlier, had warned him about the city's drivers. "He told me I was crazy to want to rent a car," Victor whispered. "He said I wouldn't get out of Paris alive."

The Ermitage Hôtel sat on its own at the top of the hill, tucked into the shadow of the church whose white dome sits above the Paris cityscape like a baker's hat. I had discovered it inside a cheap-sleeps guide to Paris, listed under the category of small romantic hotels. In all my years of coming to Paris, it was one of the few times I was staying in a hotel. I no longer had any friends in Paris with whom to stay, but I thought of that visit as a new beginning, just as my impending marriage was a new beginning, as the taxi came to a halt on the Rue Lamarck. The street was named for the 18th-century French naturalist who originated an early theory about evolution. I thought that appropriate. This trip was about my own evolution, about my growing independence and how painful that process sometimes felt.

There was another coincidence, unnoticed until I saw the brass plate on the outside wall embossed with the hotel's name. "Ermitage" was the French word for hermitage, or place of seclusion. I hadn't thought of that when choosing the hotel, but I loved the idea of it being a refuge. During the next seven days, this was where Victor and I would lock ourselves away, exiled against the world, fortressed inside our newfound society of two. I pushed open the big wooden door and walked in, Victor behind me.

Standing just over six feet tall, Victor came into the family-run hotel carrying three bags at once in his large hands, which seemed to inflate his otherwise lean girth. When he entered the small reception area, he looked like Gulliver in the land of the Lilliputians. The furniture was small and delicate, topped by vases and other assorted knickknacks. He swerved to avoid hitting his head on the low-hanging crystal chandelier. I watched, admiring his dexterity. He was like one of those lumbering basketball players who gracefully pirouette around obstacles to make a slam dunk, against all odds. I was thinking I had netted myself quite the catch and was feeling very pleased, even smug. A man who was capable.

The proprietress, Maggie Canipel, stood behind the counter, tidying her maps of Paris into neat little piles. I approached and confirmed our reservation. We were early, having come off a transatlantic flight. I was hoping she could accommodate us before the official check-in time. *"Oui Madame!"* She was of the cheery French variety, short, with red apples for cheeks. Everything I said, she answered with a melodious singsong of a voice. *"Bien sûr Madame! Tout de suite Madame!"* I wasn't really sure that she wasn't mocking me.

She gave me the key to our room, located on the top floor of the two-storey building. There wasn't an elevator. Victor led the way up the narrow staircase wound tight as a snail's shell. Framed portraits of dukes, duchesses, queens, and kings lined walls that were painted peacock blue. With his fisherman's cap lying low on his brow, Victor nearly knocked down a few. He stopped to catch his breath. Beads of perspiration were forming on his brow, but he soldiered onward and upward, not once complaining.

It being morning, the chambermaid was changing the sheets in most of the bedrooms. She had left some of the doors open. All the rooms were festooned with floral wallpaper and matching drapes. Our room was no exception. Everything was florid. A double bed dominated the postage-stamp-sized floor. Its fuzzy coverlet was curiously gray, perhaps to offset the flaming passion of all the lovers who had ever lain there, I thought, locking the door behind me.

The bed was pushed up against a far wall, under the shuttered window with a garden view. There wasn't a closet. We had to hang our winter coats on hooks on the roseate walls. To reach the washroom, equipped with a bath, we had to navigate a slender swath of carpet that stretched between the bed and our pile of belongings.

Having a bed for a room seemed to suit Victor just fine. He flopped down upon it, unleashing a cacophony of squeaks and groans from the protesting box spring below. I had been admiring the view out our window. Paris lay at our feet. Victor motioned for me to lie next to him. "Let me get a look at you," he said.

He gave me that look again, that all-encompassing gaze that made me feel as if I was the only other person alive on this earth, that made me feel magnificently adored. It's what had first made me stop in my tracks, really take notice of him.

But when I thought of it, I realized that our first encounter could have gone entirely the other way. I had come to the party where I had met him, our meeting having been arranged by mutual friends, wearing a hairpiece that was the same dark color as my own hair but boasted a cascade of curls that fell nearly to my waist. It had seemed like a good idea at the time. I thought the hair made me look alluring, though in truth I probably looked more like an over-the-top actress from a Fellini film. I had cut my hair short when fighting my employer, and the fake hair symbolized my return to some kind of place of power. It fed my Rapunzel complex. But it was also camouflage: I still wasn't sure of my resurrection. I wanted to hide behind this hair and mask the real me. I still thought I was flawed. Each time Victor touched me that night, I was afraid the hair would fall off into his hands and he would see me as a pretender.

After he dropped me off that first night, I fell asleep worrying about what he'd think when he came to see me again, as promised, two nights later. I thought he'd be disappointed.

"Surprise!"

I had opened my apartment door, sans hairpiece, to the sound of his cheery knock, and waited to see what he'd say. I thought that maybe it would be a short date.

He stood on the threshold scrutinizing me. "You are even more beautiful than I remembered," he grinned.

I opened my door wider, and he swooped in, grabbing me by the waist and twirling me in the air. He ran his fingers through my hair, my real hair, and then he kissed me.

He was kissing me again as I lay there on the hotel bed beside him. The chambermaid knocking at our door brought us groggily back to reality. She had brought us clean towels. I was unsure as to how long we had slept. It was still light outside. An hour? Maybe more? I reached for my watch. Nine in the morning Toronto time, three in the afternoon Paris time. I went into the bathroom and threw cold water on my face. Victor was already lacing up his leather boots when I came back out. "Ready to show me Paris?" he said.

I had never stayed in Montmartre before. It was off the beaten track, at the summit of a hill Parisians call the *"butte."* It had formerly been a country village, the last to be incorporated into the city's fabric, and it still had vineyards and the odd windmill. I had toured the district during my neophyte visits to Paris, drawn by the area's reputation as a former creative hot spot. Picasso and Utrillo and Satie and Berlioz and countless other famous people had had their studios in Montmartre around the turn of the 19th century, when the rents had been cheap and the morals, reportedly, just as low. It had been exotic and debauched, at least in comparison to the rest of Paris, which was ordered and gentrified by Baron Haussmann's grand plan executed on the boulevards below, close to the Seine. In many ways Montmartre remained a geographic outcast. Certainly it was off the beaten track. If ever I went there in the past, it was only to visit Sacré-Cœur.

I exited our hotel and stood dazedly outside, wondering which way to turn.

"Left," said Victor, grabbing my hand. "Let's just see where the road takes us."

His instinct had been right. We found ourselves walking in the direction of Place du Tertre, the main square. We continued holding hands as we traversed winding streets lined by buildings so narrow they resembled a deck of cards teetering precariously on the thin edges of their foundations. Black wrought-iron lanterns pushed out from the facades on brackets with a curlicue design. Under our feet the ground was cobblestone. There were no sidewalks, so we walked in the middle of a road built originally for horses, not cars. It felt mildly subversive.

A faint buzzing drew us on ahead to where a crowd had gathered on the plaza. Trees ringed the square, and their naked branches formed a kind of overhead web, ensnaring the dreams of artists and tourists alike assembled on the square, where art was the main spectacle. Dozens of artists were there, sketching or painting work displayed for sale. On this day there was also a juggler. A small crowd had gathered around him, applauding as he threw his colored pins in the air. But Victor wasn't looking at him. He was intently watching a painter working on the portrait of a woman perched in profile on a stool before him. The artist wore a beret and a smock. He had long white hair and smoked while he worked.

A swarm of geriatric shutterbugs, released from one of the big tour buses parked nearby, closed in with their cameras. A man with an accordion played a breathy French tune. The atmosphere was noisy, silly, teeming with clichés. But Victor looked full of wonder. The dramatic character of the place had enchanted him. "I understand why my father had wanted to be here," he said.

We took a table at a café. Le Sabot Rouge, the red clog, it was called. We hadn't had anything to eat since the plane ride over, and we ordered a late lunch of salad and sandwiches. At my prodding, Victor told me more about his father. He had been an artisan who had escaped Communist Yugoslavia after staging a field trip for Belgrade art students to Paris in the 1950s. After relocating to Canada, he had specialized in hand carving the interiors of churches and synagogues. He had died in Toronto of a heart attack six years previously. His death had been an absolute shock, unsettling Victor's world. Victor said he could inexplicably cry when just thinking about his father. I hoped he wouldn't then. But he seemed eager to tell me more.

His father had learned his craft in Montenegro, where he had been born and raised in a mountaintop village, the eldest of five children. During the Second World War he had been an ardent Communist until the party captured his younger brother, eventually shooting him in the back. The reason wasn't clear. The brother had been called Vidoje, pronounced vee-do-yay, derived from the Serbian word meaning "sight." A person who sees. Victor had been named for him.

He lost that trisyllabic name on his first day in a Montreal schoolroom. The teacher couldn't pronounce it. The j sounding like a y apparently had confused her, so she changed his name to something that made sense to her. Victor. Which is what everyone learned to call him, even his own mother. I declared it a most fitting appellation. "You are my victor," I said. "The conqueror of my heart."

We left the restaurant and started to walk again, dusk falling around us. We passed the painters and stopped to look at their art. It was mostly streetscapes with Sacré-Cœur looming predictably in the background. The houses were flatly drawn and candy colored. It was what on a good day might be called naive art, but Victor didn't dismiss it. "He could have been one of those street painters," Victor said of his father, who had lived in Paris for two years, sending home money to the wife he had left behind, enabling her to grease the process by which they all eventually left the country.

He had stopped to peer inside the window of an art gallery. He remembered his father's pile of papers back home, gallery notices and reviews collected when he had lived in Paris. He had forgotten about them. I stared at him. He had more reason to be in Paris than I did. He might even have grown up in Paris if it hadn't been for that family connection in Canada. I felt my heart beating fast. That had been a close call.

He turned to look at me and seemed to read my mind. "All of what happened had to have happened for us to meet," he said. "I believe that. My uncle didn't die in vain."

We walked slowly back to our hotel. Sacré-Cœur was lit up in the dark like a lighthouse, guiding us. We came to the foot of a steep staircase and were silent as we shuffled together up the steps, holding hands. I didn't have to tell him about my family. He had already met my mother. The encounter had taken place a few weeks after I had met him, when, deep inside, I knew he was the One. I used to scoff when people would say that, the One. "How do you know?" I'd say. "You just know." It sounded like a mystery cult. Then one day I was indoctrinated.

I had been alone in my apartment, making myself an espresso. It was morning. I looked out the kitchen window at the new day. "You are going to marry Victor," declared a voice inside my head, just like that, as I was reaching for the sugar. The voice was sober, sensible, not inflamed by infatuation. I thought it a true voice, its message clear. I put the spoon in my cup and carefully began to stir, deeply aware that my life was about to change. But I wouldn't tell anyone, least of all Victor. No way. I was crazy in love, but not that crazy. I had been hurt before. Best to wait things out, keep my innermost thoughts to myself—just in case, I mused, swearing myself and that little knowing voice to secrecy.

That night Victor took me to Toronto's El Mocambo nightclub. We sat in a back booth, drinking Irish coffee to keep the chill away. "Isn't this cozy?" I remember saying. We leaned in to each other. Winter was on its way. "We'll soon be spending our first Christmas together," I added, perkily. He grew silent. Had I said something wrong?

"By next Christmas," he said after a moment, "I will have asked you to marry me."

Astonished, I quickly unloaded the contents of my heart. I told him about the voice, and that I believed it. He threw his arms around me. Within seconds, we were both laughing and dabbing eyes filled with tears of joy. We had found each other! Imagine! Soul mates! I felt like a winning contestant on *Let's Make A Deal*. I was berserk with happiness at having chosen the right door and won the prize. It was so special, so important, that on the spot I made him promise not to tell another soul. At least for a year, which was when he'd said he'd propose to me for real, so as not to jinx it, I said. Victor agreed. That secret was our bond. But not for long. Less than a month later he spontaneously proposed, saying he couldn't wait any longer. He gave me a diamond ring; I gave him a promise for eternity.

SEEING AS WE were declaring undying love for each other, it was time he met my mother. I had delayed the meeting for as long as I could, but I could no longer avoid the inevitable. When I called her, I coolly told her I had met someone. "And?" she had said, sarcasm rising in her voice. "And, well, I think he's very special," I said. "I want you to meet him." She paused. "So, who is he?" I didn't want to give too much away. I was afraid she might be critical, carelessly pop my balloon. She said she'd meet us at an uptown piano bar where she used to go in the 1980s, when life as she remembered it had been good. My mother hadn't survived the recession, but Centro had. It was still considered a posh restaurant, whose subterranean bar was a favorite of Toronto's power elite. You ate $50 steaks there. You wore designer clothing. You flashed your jewelry. It was where on occasion my mother still liked to go to make her feel, as she put it, "like my life might be turning around again."

When we arrived, my mother was already nestled inside a leather banquette, nursing a large glass of Italian red wine.

She was swaying to the music and calling out to the piano player to play her song, "My Young and Foolish Heart." He was a black man with seemingly boneless fingers. He obliged her, and she sang along, a regular Doris Day. I looked at Victor with dread in my eyes.

"Just as long as I can look at you, I'm happy," he said. "Really. It will be all right." I led him toward his future mother-in-law.

"Mother, this is Victor. Victor, this is—"

"Call me Sylvia," she said, flashing him a wink. How peculiar, I thought. With everyone else I ever introduced to her she was always "Mrs." She thumped the banquette. "Slide on in," she said. "What are you drinking?" Victor moved in beside her. I took the chair on the outside of the booth, on the aisle.

I had warned Victor that my mother was in a category of her own. I hadn't wanted to tell him too much, in case we waded into some unpleasantness. I hadn't wanted to scare him off. I told him only that she could be unpredictable, which on that night she was. Meaning surprisingly well behaved. Every story she told was about her, but Victor was a rapt listener and he flattered her with his attention. Soon she was touching his arm and being coquettish. She was laughing, the life of the party. She ordered another round before we had finished our first. When Victor momentarily excused himself, she leaned in conspiratorially across the table. "I love him already," she said. But the good vibes didn't last, especially after she found out I was marrying him. "He's soft," she shouted. "Like your father. And he doesn't have a bloody job. You'll be sorry, my girl. You'll be sorry." My mother might have seen a resemblance to my father, but I did not. Victor had just been awarded a PhD in cultural anthropology from the University of Toronto. He didn't have a teaching position yet, but I knew that would come.

WHEN WE FINALLY arrived back at our hotel, after sitting for a while at the top of the stairs watching the moon crest in the night sky, we crawled quickly under the sheets to hold each other tight. "Victor?" I said. I wanted to tell him something, or maybe I just needed reassurance. But he didn't answer me. He was already asleep, still holding my hand.

The next morning we had breakfast in our room—café au lait and warm baguette. It satisfied me, but Victor was used to a Canadian breakfast. He had a hungry man's appetite and wanted ham and eggs, so we left the Ermitage and searched for a bistro.

We found one, located opposite the Lamarck-Caulaincourt metro station, toward the bottom of the hill. It was filled with locals, not tourists. Mirrors lined the walls, and a brass rail girdled the bar. Light reflected off the shiny surfaces, making the interior glow. It was a neighborhood place, intimate and charming. It wasn't quite noon, but a boisterous group, colleagues, I imagined, out for an office lunch, was already ordering *kir*. I watched the pigeon-chested waiter take their order. In his large, veined hands, he cradled a bottle of sauvignon blanc, which he seemed to rock back and forth as if it were a baby. With solemnity he poured streams of the honey-colored wine into a row of glasses on a paper-lined communal table. A patron noisily dragged up a chair and asked the waiter a question, on a point of connoisseurship, no doubt. The waiter puffed out his chest as he prepared to answer. With pursed lips and heavy eyes that seemed to have seen it all, he intoned that sauvignon blanc was the only grape variety suitable for making *kir*. Its dryness was a counterpoint to the sweet-ness of the cassis giving the aperitif its faint blush of color. *Et voilà!* It was too early for me to drink, but I made a mental note to always drink *kir*, and *kir* made this way. It would transport me back in time to that little place, that pompous waiter, those hungry people, and Victor, sitting opposite me, digging into his food, not a care in the world.

The lunch crowd also dug in, tearing at their crusty bits of bread, slurping their steaming soup, tossing the shells from their garlicky *moules* into bowls at the center table. I looked at Victor, hunched hungrily over his food. In that moment he seemed so uncomplicated. A guy who fed his hunger. I wondered if that was why I was attracted to him. I felt the grip of his hand on mine and reeled from the peppery smell of him as he drew me close. A lump rose in my throat; I felt the rawest kind of love for this man. I was so grateful for him. Oh sweet Mother of God, don't let me blow it.

"Let's settle our bill," I said.

We left the place that we instantly started calling "our" bistro, returning there daily, and headed for the metro station across the street. We descended what seemed an endless flight of stairs to reach the trains, and sat necking on the platform as we waited for one to whisk us away. Enormous sexy advertisements were postered all over the walls. Urban wallpaper. One was declaring the return of the eternal feminine. *Le retour de l'eternel féminin.* That would be me. I repeated the words like an incantation.

The train was filled with people, and we had to stand because no seats were available. We swooshed through the darkness, rocked by the train's forward motion. I loved the Paris metro. It anchored me. It was a large part of my Paris experience. How many times had I intently studied the map, a large net of crisscrossing lines and knots cut almost in half by the snaking figure of the Seine. There were more than a dozen routes and about three hundred stations, most no more than a quarter mile apart. I loved reading their names: Abbesses, Pigalle, Saint-Georges, Notre-Dame-de-Lorette, Saint-Lazare, Auber, Madeleine. The words were like beads on a rosary. You counted them in anticipation of a divine time in a city made up of so many variables. With each stop the train filled with more people. We were squeezed in together, Victor's fingers interlocking with mine as we tried to hold on to the back of one of the seats. No one was talking.

We allowed our eyes to wander, the ride affording us a chance to examine the Parisians up close. Students in tight jeans listening to Walkmans. Men with briefcases and that morning's edition of *Le Monde* in hand. Lolitas perfecting their pouts. Perfectly coiffed matrons fingering jewel-toned leather gloves folded neatly on cashmere laps. What I didn't realize was that people on the train were also looking at us. "We stand out," Victor whispered into my ear. "Paris is supposed to be a romantic city, but I don't see anyone else holding hands. Everyone's rushing by, going where they're going alone. Except for us."

I imagined they looked at us with envy. We were the ones in love. In Paris that was a position of high status. Victor and I exited at Pont Neuf. Outside, we crossed the old bridge, pausing to peer down into the river. The Seine was thick and turbulent. I had forgotten how elemental a force it was, carving Paris into left bank and right bank geographies and mindsets. At that moment we stood on the Rive Droite, surrounded by three-hundred-year-old mansions and *pâtisseries* with origami-like cakes in their windows. Barges were moored along the banks beside houseboats. A nip was in the air. I shivered in my heavy black Canadian coat, thinking that it must be dreadfully cold to live on one of those boats, especially in the winter, and I drew closer to Victor, who wrapped his bearish arms around me.

"I want to get a feel for the rhythms of Paris, the walking, the driving, the gesticulating, the motion of the metro, the speed of a cab—the everyday life of a city," he said. "And I want to do that with my arm clasped around your waist."

We walked along the way toward Île Saint-Louis, one of my favorite places, and sauntered down genteel streets lined with elegant, old buildings. The air grew still, and there was very little traffic. The island felt like a oasis of intimacy. We walked softly together, ruminating and sharing thoughts and observations, not always about Paris, but about ourselves, our likes and dislikes, what we had experienced in the past, our zeal for the future. Thought flowed with the river. With Victor I felt boundless. Weightless. With him, I didn't walk through Paris, I floated.

We turned a corner, drifting past historic churches and artifact shops that Victor didn't want to enter. Museum-going wasn't as high on his agenda as it was on mine. "There are different ways of getting to know a city," he said. His idea of a good time in the French capital was being out of doors and exploring together the avenues, the quiet of a bench under a tree in a park. He said he wanted to talk and revel in the physicality of being in love.

We walked onward, but, not being able to help myself, being a bit of a Paris pedant, I pointed out the building where Baudelaire had once lived. The poet had once organized a small society of hashish smokers inside those walls, I said, regurgitating something I had once read. Victor stopped and kissed me. He was the real intellectual but he knew how to live in the present. He knew how to be. "Just relax," he whispered.

I held onto his hand as I led him across Pont Saint-Louis toward the Île de la Cité. We were on the bridge, behind Notre Dame. Massive, with its stone beams, or buttresses, supporting the weight of its roof, the cathedral looked like a butterfly with outspread wings. Victor asked to stop for a moment to admire its rare beauty, at once delicate and imposing. We continued walking and ended up on the Quai Saint-Michel to stroll along the river and browse through the bookstalls. He inspired in me a slower pace.

The dampness in the air penetrated our bones. We needed to seek shelter and a hot cup of coffee. I suggested we go to La Samaritaine, the art nouveau department store on the riverbank, where I had once come looking for self-transformation at one of the makeup counters. I remembered an upstairs café whose terrace afforded a 360-degree view of Paris. It was perfect for a first-time visitor, or even a seasoned one, to savor the city's diversity. Victor said to lead the way.

We rode an old wooden escalator to an upper floor and went out onto the terrace. The day was clear, with a few snowy clouds veiling the air. I looked down and saw Paris spread out beneath us for miles, an assortment of architectural styles and shapes. But from that distance, high in the sky, Paris looked uniformly white, as if carved from a single slab of vanilla limestone. It must have been my state of mind, but Paris in that moment looked like a bride to me. It made me think that it was a sign, somehow. My marriage would be strong, as Paris was strong. It would endure, as Paris has endured. Everything would be okay.

I drew closer to Victor and pointed out the mighty dome of the Panthéon, a former church that was secularized during the French Revolution and that rose high above Paris. The circular roof sat on a ring of slender columns and topping it was a plinthlike structure studded with a sky-piercing crucifix. It looked like an upside-down ice cream cone. The mausoleum, I told Victor, housed the remains of Voltaire, Rousseau, and Descartes, the great intellectuals of France. I had been inside on an earlier visit, and described the pastel-colored paintings by Puvis de Chavannes that lined the walls. It hadn't occurred to me before, but in recalling their airy imagery, I said that the paintings lent that temple of the dead a feeling of spring-time and joy.

There were several other domes on the horizon, making Paris look like a camel of many humps. One belonged to Sacré-Cœur, looming hazily in the distance. I pointed it out, enabling Victor to appreciate just how far we had travelled from the hill of Montmartre to where we then stood, at the center of Paris. But Victor was more interested in locating another domed landmark, the Sorbonne, where his grandfather on his mother's side had attended philosophy classes at the beginning of the century. It was just beyond the river, near the Cluny museum off the Boulevard Saint-Michel, rolling out beneath us like a satin ribbon. Its spherical roof, topped by a cross, was easy to find. Smaller than the Panthéon's, the Sorbonne's dome was decorated with a series of small eyelike windows carved into the exterior, giving the ancient university an air of wisdom, its gaze unblinkingly focused on the world around it.

Next we turned to look at the *Arc de Triomphe*, looking like the hub of a giant wheel with streets radiating outward like spokes from its center. I thought of the many times I had walked there, up and down the Champs-Élysées, into side streets sheltering acrid tobacco shops, *bureaux de tabac*, and old but familiar cafés. I thought of the times I had wandered there alone, feeling lost in thought if not in purpose. I remembered that Paris, on previous trips, had sometimes made me feel alienated, isolated, alone. I felt Victor's arm around my shoulders, holding me tight. There was a logic to Paris when seen from above, close to the clouds. The streets had an obvious order that made them easy, all of a sudden, to navigate. I told Victor we should go back down into the city to explore it for ourselves.

Earlier Victor had said that he found museums sterile, full of objects that lacked what Paris had heightened in him, a craving for human contact. But he wanted to see the

Louvre. We headed in the direction of the world's most celebrated museum by strolling beneath the canopied arcade of the Palais Royal. There was a new entrance, I.M. Pei's glass pyramid, still controversial since its 1989 unveiling. Traditionalists were calling it a blight on the face of Paris, but I saw it as a sign that Paris changed with the times. I liked how the pyramid's ancient shape blended with the antique splendor of the former palace of kings.

I had assumed we would do all of the museum's greatest hits, the *Venus de Milo*, the *Mona Lisa*, the windblown *Winged Victory of Samothrace*, forever standing guard over the well-trodden marble staircase inside. But Victor didn't care for the Italian masterpieces or the French paintings and Greek statuary that made the Louvre so famous. He was interested in its cache of Sumerian and Assyrian artifacts from the region that is modern-day Iraq. He wanted to go back to the beginning of Western civilization, to understand how we got from there to here. Paris, he said, was having that kind of effect on him.

A free museum map in hand, we stood in the underground entranceway of the new Louvre and together looked for the Richelieu wing, where the Oriental antiquities were housed. It was an area of the museum I didn't know very well—and I thought I knew the museum inside out.

We found the rooms dedicated to the Fertile Crescent, the basin between the Tigris and Euphrates rivers. I had studied ancient Mesopotamia in grade 7, when I was thirteen, in my first year at the girls' school my mother had insisted on sending me to. I remembered my teacher, Mrs. Rachlis, a bespectacled and earnest woman with a helmet of inky-black hair that overpowered her wraithlike frame. She spoke with a lisp but managed to thunder out each syllable in the *Codex Hammurabi*, inspiring in us girls a feeling of awe. That was the first time I had heard of the Babylonian king and lawmaker. I hadn't given him much thought since, but Victor was excitedly looking for signs of his legacy. He found Hammurabi immortalized in the black basalt stela that contained his code, hammered into 3,500 lines containing 282 laws, each defining an aspect of moral and ethical conduct within society. The *Codex* had originated the concept of a tooth for a tooth, an eye for an eye, justice for when things went wrong.

I looked around for Victor, but he had moved on and was standing before an enormous stone plinth with the title *Stele of the Vultures*. I drew closer to see what he was seeing: An army of helmeted soldiers battering the enemy underfoot. Corpses piled high, birds of prey swooping down to pick the flesh off their bones. A tethered ox being led to sacrifice; the king in his chariot in a victory parade. Cuneiform running across the base, recounting the whole bloody story. "All civilizations are begot by blood baths," Victor said, paraphrasing Walter Benjamin. "It is why wars are waged, to impose a community's cultural values at the expense of another's."

Continuing through galleries representing two thousand years of ancient history, I saw that what he said was true. Almost all the artwork vividly documented how each civilization killed the one that came before; it seemed to be the only way a new era could blossom. The Sumerians were knocked off by the Akkadians, followed by the Assyrians, who were in turn destroyed by the Babylonians. As I stood in the vast throne room of Sargon II, a king of Nineveh, dwarfed by colossal statues of winged bulls with human heads that had once guarded an ancient palace, I wondered if that was not just the way of the world. In marrying this man, I would be replacing my mother as the most influential person in my life, in order to allow a new stage in my life to take root. That was a natural process, I reasoned, part of the cycle of life. But I hadn't anticipated this rite of passage to be so fraught with aggression. I hadn't foreseen a battle. As my wedding day drew nearer, my mother would fight me tooth and nail. She would scream, call me names, slam down the phone, brand me a traitor. "You're the kind of female who dumps her girlfriend for a guy," she hissed. Except she wasn't my girlfriend.

We left the Louvre and walked through the Jardin des Tuileries. Hunger motivated us to keep walking in search of a restaurant. We found one just on the other side of the gardens, near the Place de la Concorde, called L'Épi d'Or, the golden sword. It was dimly lit, with barrelled walls, something of a cave. Everyone sat knee to knee at a long communal table, where Victor and I shared a cake swimming in Calvados. Surreptitiously, he started caressing my thighs. A French man sharing the bench with us looked at Victor and then looked intently at me. He understood what was going on. He sighed and continued eating his dinner. Before leaving, he bought us a nightcap, without saying a word. Just a tip of the hat.

Our tiny hotel room soon became an everywhere, and over the next few days we hardly left it to venture back into Paris. The city's spirit had infected us, making us feel invincible. Madame Canipel left breakfast outside our door.

Paris, once we returned to it after a day and night of intimate seclusion, seemed to lack the intensity of our time in the hotel room. We went to Trocadéro Square to watch the skateboarders. We visited Napoleon's marble tomb at Les Invalides and swung dizzily around lampposts lining Boulevard Saint-Germain, laughing as we fell into each other's arms. We watched the sunset from the steps of Sacré-Cœur. But nothing could approximate our state of grace. And then we stumbled upon the perfect complement to our feelings of being transported by love: the graveyards of Paris.

It wasn't planned. It was the result of waking up too late after our nights of lovemaking to get into any of the monuments that we might have wanted to visit during our final days in Paris. And it was a result of Victor's plan to just wander about and see what we might see. We couldn't have found anything more life affirming. Love is an emblem of eternity, as Madame de Staël has said. It confounds all notions of time, effaces all memory of a beginning, all fear of an end. The graveyards of Paris symbolized this sentiment for us, and we took to wandering in them daily to commune with the spirits of the dead. The Montmartre cemetery was close to the hotel. We discovered it one day after eating a *croque-monsieur* at our bistro and strolling down the Boulevard de Clichy. We entered within its stone walls, not knowing what we'd find. But there, among the hillocks and the crumbling tombstones, some dating back to the cemetery's founding in 1798, were the graves of the great choreographer Vaslav Nijinsky and the Romantic-era ballerina Marie Taglioni, and of Edgar Degas and Émile Zola, artists I admired. It was a serendipitous discovery. The day was overcast, and the burial grounds were empty except for these specters animating my imagination.

Inspired, the following day Victor and I headed for Père-Lachaise with an agenda to find the artists who had played a role in shaping who we were, who had stoked our dreams of creativity when we were young. For Victor it was Chopin. Victor had been a piano student in his youth, playing Chopin in competition. He associated the composer with the depths and heights of feeling. "It's what Paris, and being in love, is stirring within me," he said, holding me close. For me, the artist was Oscar Wilde, the stylishly subversive poet of my stormy adolescence. Each recalled to us the glory of their art, which had survived them beyond the grave. Each reminded us of a mutually held belief in art as not just a thing, but a way. Oscar Wilde had said that the secret of life is in art. And standing before his tombstone inside Père-Lachaise, I understood his words to mean that art was the tangible dream. It was a lot like love in that regard: a world uplifted by desire.

Several times in the past I had come to Père-Lachaise looking for Wilde's tombstone, an art deco sculpture by Jacob Epstein, which I knew from photographs in books. But I had never been able to find it. I had always come to the cemetery by myself, and, while I had purchased a map of the graveyard beforehand at one of the flower shops beyond the perimeter, I could never find my way. Without fail, I would end up at the grave of Jim Morrison, tripping over the ragtag group of mourners who always seemed to be lighting a reefer in memory of his rock-and-roll spirit. They were there still. But this time was different.

Victor had the same confounding map in hand, but he read it better than I could. He knew which way to go, as he had the whole time we were in Paris. He knew how to lead me on the right path. And so, after nearly fifteen years of trying and failing, I found Oscar Wilde at long last.

And alien tears will fill for him
Pity's long-broken urn
For his mourners will be outcast men,
And outcasts always mourn.

We read the inscription on his monument together and imagined the musician of words singing in the wind that whipped through the silence carpeting Père-Lachaise. Victor shared my feeling for him. He appreciated his genius. "Yet each man kills the thing he loves," he said to me with a wink, as I leaned forward to kiss the cold stone, my lipstick merging with all the other lipstick farewells staining the tomb. "Thank-you," I said. I reached for Victor's hand, to draw him near. I was ready to start my new life with him. He had passed the test.

Later that night we strolled for the last time around Montmartre. I had bought Victor a pewter flask a few weeks earlier for Christmas. He had brought it with him to Paris. At a corner store he purchased a bottle of brandy, and he carefully transferred the contents. The air was nippy, and we drank as we walked, to warm our insides. We were back on Clichy, moving east from the Place Blanche toward Pigalle. Refuse was strewn about the dingy boulevard. Prostitutes lolled in doorways, horns blared rudely, facades were thick with grime. Gentrification had missed this part of Paris, and the neighborhood had the stench of authenticity about it—putrid and sour. The Montmartre of old, still a geographical outcast.

We sat on a street bench to absorb the view. It felt cozy snuggling up against each other, our love creating a shelter against the effluvium of the street bubbling around us. We took furtive sips from the flask. We weren't sure if public consumption of alcohol was permitted. In Toronto, we would have been arrested. But we soon noticed that the neighborhood was littered with characters grasping bottles to their chests to keep themselves from catching their deaths. They wobbled when they walked, or else fell straight down onto the sidewalk in drunken heaps. Victor and I laughed at the thought of us as two Parisian winos. It made us think of George Orwell's *Down and Out in Paris and London,* a book documenting the author's 1929 stay in Paris, when he was penniless, friendless, and regarded as a scourge of society because he was poor. He wrote of men broken by indigence; of the physical, moral, and mental degradation that accompanies extreme need. And while documenting the worst of humanity, he also celebrated the resilience of the human spirit. He showed how humans can endure hardship and be transformed by it.

As I huddled close to Victor on that bench, observing the bob and weave of Paris's army of *inconnus,* I recalled being on this same stretch of street when I was nineteen, alarmed by the transvestites walking in broad daylight in high heels and torn black stockings. I had dismissed them at that time as freaks.

But now I was in love, and I regarded these creatures of the night with more tolerance and affection than before. Love was waging in me a revolution of inner change. I felt empowered, as if with Victor I could take on the world and anyone that would sever our bond.

I asked Victor for another swig of brandy, a toast to reform. The night sky above Paris was bursting with stars. I felt the drink burn as it trickled down my throat. Baptism by fire.

I HAD THE first of my two children in October 1999 and, after a yearlong maternity leave, returned to work to find that I had a new job. I was suddenly and without warning my newspaper's new fashion reporter. The woman who had held the position before me had recently quit, taking an editorship position at a Toronto-based magazine. There could be no outside hire to replace her, as a hiring freeze was in effect at the newspaper in the fall of 2000.

"So you're it," said the new department head, smiling at me as I sat opposite her on a sagging sofa inside her top-floor office.

I remember I was wearing a silk blouse, periwinkle blue, and at that moment, likely because of the shock of her pronouncement, I leaked breast milk. It was just a few drops, but enough to create an ever-widening circle on my chest.

"Why me?" I stammered. I hadn't applied for the job and felt I had no qualifications.

"Look at you!" she exclaimed, eyeing me up and down. "You love clothes!"

I felt momentarily chagrined. Since my marriage in the fall of 1995 I had pushed to reinvent myself, not just in my personal life, but also at work, where I had carved out a new niche as an investigative arts reporter. I had been specializing in art fraud, working with police and the RCMP in outing crooked dealers and art thieves, some of whom I was responsible for getting arrested. Just before I went on maternity leave, I had also broken a story about a major labor dispute involving the National Ballet of Canada and one of its ousted ballerinas. My coverage sparked a nationwide debate about the role of artistic directors in our politically correct times. Could they still hire and fire at will? On my return, I expected to resume the tough assignments. I had proven myself. And so I was taken aback, really thrown, when I was told that after all that hard work in the trenches, I would instead be writing about clothes. It felt like a put-down, a slap in the face. While my boss beamed at me, I was seriously contemplating whether or not I should quit.

"Of course, you'll get to travel," said my editor, breaking into my thoughts. "New York. Milan. Paris."

At the sound of that word, Paris, I snapped to my senses.

"Paris?" I said to her, my eyes widening. "You will be sending me to Paris? To work?" My editor is a shrewd woman with an uncanny ability to rule even the most recalcitrant reporter. I had previously seen her bring big burly news guys to their knees. She held my attention completely.

"Of course you'll be covering the Paris collections," she said, leaning forward in her chair. She was going in for the kill. "With your investigative skills and innate love of clothes, you're going to put fashion on the front page. We're going to make you a star! When you say something's in, it's in!"

Vanity, thy name is a front-row seat at Louis Vuitton. I forgot all about resistance and nodded stupidly at her as the wet spot on my shirt grew bigger and brighter. Yes. Me. In Paris. A star. And with Paris now doing the calling.

"Okay." I exhaled. "So when do I start packing my bags?"

I floated back to my desk and emailed my husband to tell him what had just transpired, emphasizing the star part. "New baby, new career, it all harmonizes," I wrote, launching effortlessly into fashionspeak. My boss was right; I was a natural. How could I not be, given that my mother had always made sure I was the best-dressed kid at school, her little show pony. I had grown up loving dresses and having my hair done just so.

Yet my manager's appointing of me meant that there were snubbed noses in the department, women who had spent their lives cultivating a love of fashion into a news-paper job. There I was, to their minds a know-nothing, if not a know-it-all, parachuted in above them, given the visible push. My mail was opened, and invitations to local fashion events discarded in the trash. A leading Canadian fashion designer asked me to visit him at his studio, where he told me to watch my back. "The knives are out," he twittered, fluffing one of his trademark skirts made of cit-rusy tulle. "People call you the Dragon Lady," he added, thrillingly. *Moi?*

If I had an air of fierceness about me, it was probably because for the last five years, ever since my marriage, I continued to be engaged in low-intensity warfare with my mother. Except now it was worse than ever. She attacked me constantly, finding fault in how I kept house and, lately, in how I was raising my son. "I'm watching you," she said in the weeks following my son's birth. "And I can see you haven't a clue. You have to leave Victor and come live with me. It's clear that I have to take over, to give the baby a proper start."

When I told her that was patently ridiculous, that I wasn't leaving my husband's side or handing over my child, she erupted into a vicious tirade that concluded with her refusing to see or talk to me for most of a year. Which meant she also turned her back on her grandson, which I found hard to forget and even harder to forgive. I felt angry but unable to express it.

It was an attitude I brought with me into the workplace, cutting through resentment with a steely determination to be the best at what I did, working extra-long hours, sometimes until two in the morning. It was a punishing schedule and it didn't make me any friends. I was hurting inside, but to others I seemed stiff and unapproachable. The fashion editor took to calling me diva. It wasn't a compliment.

I soldiered through the jealousy by fixing my sights on Paris. I was going there, and they weren't. Everyone, I imagined, salivated for a bit of Paris, wonderful by way of a hemline report. Up or down? And I was the one chosen to give it. It was an empowering feeling. On a more personal note, I still viewed Paris as the Emerald City, that illusory ideal where I could learn style, poise, become a real-life *parisienne* after all these years. My very own finishing school. Many of the girls that I had met in my junior years at private school had gone to Switzerland and come back trilling French, wearing extra layers of fat thanks to all the expensive pastries they had consumed. I had always wanted that for myself—not the extra calories but a fancy French education. I wondered if that was what Paris had always represented to me. The chance to gain sophistication first hand? Certainly, in going to Paris this time around, I envisioned myself as Cinderella in her glass coach, wearing magical clothes, emerging as the belle of the ball, against all odds. That was the image that sprang to mind as soon as my editor had said that captivating word, Paris.

But that was the view from afar. Being in Paris to cover the shows was another story. Just because my publication had ordered me to cover the collections and was willing to cover the cost of a transatlantic flight and ten days in a three-star Paris hotel, about a $5,000 expenditure, didn't mean I could. Before I even stepped onto an airplane that would take me to the 2001–02 fall/winter ready-to-wear collections, staged throughout Paris in February of that year, I had to engage in months of pre-arrival preparations. First I had several forms to fill out, forms identifying my organization and me, forms that needed to be signed by me, my editor, my editor's editor, the editor-in-chief, and finally the publisher himself. If I had clippings demonstrating coverage of past collections, I was urged to send them along, as this could favorably influence the Féderation française de la couture, the trade group that is the mafia of French fashion. It would be the one to stamp *oui* or *non* on my application. After several weeks' wait, fraught with uncertainty, I finally got word that I was a *oui*. I was accredited. I was off to Paris to see the shows. Or so I thought.

Even accredited, I couldn't get into the collections unless personally invited by the designer or members of his or her entourage. They had to want me to be at their individual shows, each lasting an average of fifteen minutes and costing upward of $1 million to stage. It was all part of a Paris institution I hadn't been aware of before, *la liste*. If you weren't on it, your only hope of reporting on Paris fashion was out on the street. Or so I learned on my first day as a fashion reporter in Paris, spent tediously dialling the numbers of snooty press attachés to ask them, in my very best French, if they would grant me the honor of an invitation to one of their theatrical fashion spectacles.

One in particular belonged to Viktor & Rolf, the Dutch design duo who were then considered the last word in avant-garde fashion. Very wow. I had never heard of them, but everyone was talking about how edgy they were. And so, sitting inside my Left Bank hotel, a converted monastery girded by large brick walls dating back to the Middle Ages, I rang up the rep to ask for an invite.

"But I dunt know yu," said the woman on the other end of the phone, breaking into English, a sign that my French was bad.

"What do you mean?" I said.

"We dunt 'ave a relationship," she responded.

"And how do we have a relationship?" I asked.

"You cum to ze showroom to look at ze clothes, and I look at you looking at zem, to know if I will give you an invitation for next year."

"But I don't want an invitation for next year, I want an invitation for this year, I am in Paris now," I said, frustration mounting in my voice.

"But zis is ze situation," she replied. I could feel her shrug of Gallic indifference at the other end of the phone line.

"*Ce n'est pas un jeu, Madame,* this is not a game," I said, starting to shout, "My newspaper has spent a lot of money sending me to Paris. I must get into the show this week."

"But zis is not *mon problème,*" she said. And hung up on me.

I sat in that expensive boutique hotel room, big as a walk-in closet, and stared at my reflection in a wall mirror. My hair was lank, my eyes hollow. I looked tired. I hadn't even attended my first show, but already Paris fashion felt like *Les Misèrables* come to life. I was trying to storm the barricades of French arrogance, to no avail. I would have to grovel before I could penetrate the city's fabled gardens of beauty. Clearly I had much to learn. I tried explaining to the fashion editor, the one left sorely behind in Toronto, that I was having a bit of difficulty gaining access to the shows. "Hey," she barked, cutting me off. "It's Paris, not a war zone. Stop complaining." She was right. It wasn't a war zone. At least in a war you know who the enemy is. This was subterfuge. The point in denying the press access was to create an air of exclusivity around a particular fashion brand. It was also designed to whip up a feeling of frenzy among the fashion disenfranchised. Certainly that was the sensation being roused in me. The more they didn't let me in, the more determined I was to get in. I opened my suitcase and pulled out a new red dress, purchased especially for the trip. I would beat the Parisians at their own game, I thought. I would dress to kill. I was forty years old. I didn't need to put up with this shit.

I left the subdued elegance of the Hôtel de l'Abbaye on Rue Cassette and headed for the nearby Rue de Rennes, puffed like a revolutionary, eager to put the tiny heads of my fashion foes on the spiky end of a pole. I strode across Boulevard Saint-Germain, oblivious to the motorcycles that swerved to avoid hitting me. I crossed the Seine, kicking at the pigeons pecking at crumbs on the bridge. I wanted to push through anything in my way, especially the barricades of snobbery that Paris had erected to guard the sanctity of its fashion shows from the likes of uncouth North Americans like myself.

Most of the shows were held inside the Louvre within the subterranean Carrousel pedestrian mall. I rode down the escalators into the bowels of the museum and saw uniformed security guards. They weren't there for the artwork. They were there for the fashion, protecting it from intruders. I saw metal detectors and X-ray machines such as you'd encounter at the airport. In Paris, fashion was serious business. You didn't just bust in unannounced.

I had my press pass, and with a nod of his head a guard with a holster on his hip granted me access to the media lounge. It was a white-leather and chrome oasis, pulsating with disco music. Sundry journalists sat on überchic plastic bar stools, quaffing bottles of Evian. I didn't know anyone. But fashion being a perk-laden beat, the drinks were free, the food was free, and so was the hairstyling and makeup application by the professional team from L'Oréal, the main sponsor of the show. It was set up to make anyone who entered feel part of an ersatz tribe. I was in need of belonging. A team of young women with dazzlingly white smiles approached and, like Sirens, called to me to try out all the wonders of their beauty-charged world. It was such a reversal from the Nazi PR people I had been fighting with all morning over the phone. One had informed me point blank that the reason I wouldn't be getting an invitation to the Christian Dior show was because I was a Canadian. "And *le Canada* is not *exactement* a fashion country, *non?*" He had elaborated on the national stereotype by telling me that no matter how adulatory I might be of the show, I wouldn't be helpful in selling much Christian Dior product. Canada was not known for being a nation of luxury fashion spenders. "So why should we let you in?" His words had annoyed me. Until that point I had prided myself on being a journalist who was above caring about commercial interests. I was an independent, a champion of the underdog. The truth will out, and all that. But fashion was a new world. It wasn't just about appearances, it was about money. To momentarily forget about the ugly underbelly of Paris fashion, I allowed myself to be enchanted by all the gratuitous opportunities for self-improvement, and tried them all, starting with a free glass of French champagne.

Over the next few days I returned frequently to the Louvre, my "office," and became a veritable Hoover of all the free stuff that befell me at the fashion shows—the graft. Most of the big designers decorated the chairs of the press with little goody bags in which were eyeliners and lip pencils, real French perfume, or sunglasses. It was meant to buy you, buy your precious objective soul. For the most part it worked. Overnight, I became a fashion victim. I imagined that Valentino himself had personally placed gifts in my path, and this made me feel like an intimate, a member of the fashion elite. I believed that I was suddenly oh-so-fabulous, too. And so the fashion world sucked me in and sprinkled me with fairy dust. Soon I was getting my hair blown out daily and buying $100 orange leather booties for my toddler at the deluxe department store Bon Marché. I walked down the Rue du Faubourg Saint-Honoré wearing a new purple coat edged in marabou. If my mother could see me now, I thought, catching my reflection in the window of the Hermès boutique.

I stood in line to get inside the next fashion show of the day, glad for the distraction of work. It was Celine. Or was it Lanvin? It was all beginning to blur. I needed to focus. I was in Paris, after all, in search of the Trend. It was all about the Trend. And that season, it looked like a purse.

A bone-handled clutch by Yves Saint Laurent, to be precise. Absolutely de rigueur. One woman, Carine Roitfeld, the highly influential editor-in-chief of Paris *Vogue,* was responsible for branding it into the collective fashion consciousness as the accessory du jour, carrying it with her all the time, like a shield. Muse to Tom Ford, the chief designer of Yves Saint Laurent as well as Gucci in Milan, fashion's Amazon queen was a regular at the shows. When she entered the tents where the events took place, the paparazzi flew after her, cameras flashing. Sometimes she arrived with her pretty daughter on her arm. I found myself wondering about their relationship. Did they share each other's clothes? That was something mothers and daughters often did. I used to borrow my mother's, but not anymore.

I shook my head clear it, to concentrate on Madame Roitfeld. What made her tick? What was her allure? To me, she was an enigma, the sphinx of the fashion shows. She rimmed her sunken eyes with inky kohl, making her look like a raccoon. Every day she persisted in wearing the same clothes, as if brazenly repudiating the fashion merry-go-round swirling around us, in which each 20-minute show typically showcased up to 130 different looks at a time. It was as if she was saying, why bother? She had found her uniform of chic. That season it consisted of a black shawl, a black midcalf skirt, and, despite the fact that it was February and still chilly outside, a pair of black, open-toe, wraparound, stacked-heel sandals, the shoe destined to become *the* shoe of the summer of 2001, and all because *she* wore it.

I looked closer. She was rail thin, and her hair was a bird's nest. Whispers followed in her wake. She was said to be the progenitor of heroin chic. She was said to be like Colette, culling lovers from both sexes. But she wasn't what you'd call good-looking. Instead, she epitomized what at the beginning of the new millennium was being recast as the new glamor—a quirky individuality that mixed summer sandals with winter shawls, plastic bracelets with gold earrings as big as basketball hoops. Some of Paris's moneyed matrons also sat in the front row of the fashion shows, sternly eyeing Madame Roitfeld. Their handbags were small and color-coded to match their outfits. They looked staid in comparison to Madame Roitfeld. She emerged the winner. I learned more about Paris's enduring reputation as the incubator of new fashion by observing her than by watching ten full days of shows. She represented a whole new topsy-turvy sense of what it meant to be in style. If there had been rules about what it meant to be well dressed, she tossed them out the window. I glanced again at Madame Roitfeld and sighed. She made me feel impossibly bereft. I had the wrong clothes. I wondered if I would ever be a *parisienne*.

The right clothes marched down the runway on the bodies of models who high-stepped their way to the fashion photographers crammed together at the opposite end of the catwalk. Nicknamed the Grapparazzi for all the libations they typically imbibed in the morning to get them through the exhausting pace of the day, the photographers were a bastion of maleness in a world where females stealthily judged each other's grasp of style. The women were subtle. The men were not. Sexist and loud, the shooters routinely shouted, *à poil!*—French for "take it all off," to a model they wanted a second look from. It was a cat-and-mouse game, a blood sport at the center of a pretentious forum paved with expensive designer duds. It was also part of the camp entertainment offered up by the shows. You could determine the character of a girl by the way she handled the catcalls. Britain's Stella Tennant, aristocratic by birth, gave them the haughty stare. Canada's Tasha Tilberg, originally from small-town British Columbia, looked vacantly through them, frightened by the scorching attention or else just too young to know what to do. Denmark's sexy Helena Christensen licked her finger and slowly raised it in a rude salute to the animals screaming to see her tits.

The audience sat stonily observing the models, the clothes, and, in particular, each other. The Paris collections were as much about the fashions as the personalities who gathered twice yearly to pass judgment on them. Over there was the pre-op transsexual, standing monstrously taller than the rest of the stiletto-heeled crowd, flailing his manicured hands in a show of delirium over the latest John Galliano. Over here was the aging former editor of an Italian fashion magazine, rouged and plucked, a hat that looked like a tower of shellacked CDs topping her silver head of hair, and a pirate patch over one heavily made-up eye. She was short and squat, a toadlike fashion-show fixture. Next to her was the photographer of the moment, boy toy of *Vanity Fair*, legs spread wide open to show off the crown jewels bulging through his skintight designer jeans. A former American supermodel, then an overly Botoxed drunk, had just written her memoirs of sex on the catwalk and other cocaine-sprinkled capers. She was everywhere at the shows that season, having clawed her way in after the guards outside had tried to keep her from entering. At that moment she careened in a photographer's direction. He had a Polaroid camera at the ready. They air-kissed, then pretended to talk to each other, all the while eyeing the other people eyeing them.

I wished I had someone to share it all with, to share a giggle. But no one looked in my direction, least of all the legions of women standing in for the best-selling New York and British fashion magazines. They were too busy competing with each other. Each magazine upped the ante by stuffing as many bums in seats as possible. The row allotted to British *Marie Claire* seemed to have twenty people in it, and yet the magazine's masthead didn't boast as many. Who were these people? Everyone and her shar-pei seemed to have been trotted out to give a strong showing at the collections. There was the shoe editor, the handbag editor, the lipstick editor. Each with an assistant assisting an assistant. The ranks of the Americans were equally dense and mysterious. These were girls groomed within an inch of their lives, and they were the cattiest. They sneered and pouted and cavalierly tossed their handbags over their shoulders, not caring who they hit. If they didn't like their seat allotment, they snapped a finger at a clipboard operator and loudly protested. Incredibly, they got what they whined for. In fashion, politeness was for pussies. A gritty attitude earned you respect.

I tried it out. When I called for an invitation, I no longer took no for an answer. For the most part it worked. I soon had a pile of invitations waiting from me at the Hôtel de l'Abbaye, much to the annoyance of the other sad-sack Canadians also staying there, a motley crew of stylists and editors, some of whom had been trying to penetrate the Paris collections for years.

"You have an invitation to Alexander McQueen?" shrieked a freckle-faced frump from *Flare*, Canada's leading fashion magazine. I didn't, but lied. "Don't tell me you've also got one to Viktor & Rolf?"

"Not yet," I said, as sweetly as possible.

"Fuck!" she said, storming up the spiral staircase, her heels making gunfire sounds on the oak flooring.

I didn't tell her that most of my invitations had been stamped *en standing*, a third-rate category obliging members of the foreign press and other dogs of the trade to stand on tiptoe at the back of tiered rows of seats inside a stuffy, poorly lit tent. It was hard to figure out the hem lengths from that exiled point of view. All I could see were perfectly coiffed heads moving up and moving down the runway, like a brisk game of boules. Occasionally I scored a seat, usually at a has-been label like Claude Montana or Thierry Mugler. I sat in the fashion equivalent of the boonies, far away from the real fashion connoisseurs, and far from sight. In this fashion Siberia were other journos from countries with a next-to-zero fashion sensibility, at least in the eyes of the French. At Christian Lacroix, a designer whose pop-art color sense was at odds with the monochromatic looks popular that season, I was squeezed between the lone fashion reporter from Athens and the one from Bucharest. We had little in common save our ink-stained fingers. We were among the few at the shows who took any notes. Later I learned that the shortcut to writing about the shows was to crib the daily reports in the *Journal du Textile*, sold inside the tents for a few euros. It was how the other Canadians sent to Paris to cover the event wrote their summaries without actually getting in to see anything. I thought that if their publications knew, given how much it cost to send them there, they'd be fired. But I wasn't going to be the one to tell—even though I had revenge on my mind.

One morning the woman from *Flare* had organized a breakfast for fellow Canadians at the hotel. She hadn't invited me. When I walked into the dining room, they lowered their voices and cast furtive glances in my direction. I was convinced they had been talking about me. I strode up to their table, round and lined with a crisp white tablecloth. I bid them a frosty good morning. Like my mother, I wouldn't be ignored. Goddamn it. When did I become her? The woman from *Flare* looked sheepishly up at me with croissant on her blushing face. I made certain to tell her so, and then turned away to fume behind my *Herald Tribune*.

I shouldn't have minded the slight, but I did. I called my husband that night and moaned that I must be truly unlikeable. My mother, the French, my so-called colleagues, what gives? I was lying in a bath filled with a scented French oil I had purchased that afternoon. I was softening skin that my husband told me I should learn to thicken.

"I like you," he said, teasingly. "I think you are the most likeable, loveable, embraceable woman in the universe. I can't wait for you to come home, and feel my arms around you."

In a nutshell, that was my marriage. Still a sanctuary of love, five years later. I hadn't been to Paris since before we were married. I had returned there without him, and it was the first time we had been apart since our wedding day. I realized how much I missed him, how much I had grown reliant on him for company and understanding. With him I felt comfortable. With everyone else, I seemed not to fit in. "You are the only one I want to be with," I said, my eyes stinging. "You're the only one I can talk to. Paris feels lonely without you."

I don't know if I felt calmer after I woke up the next day. Maybe I had just grown numb. It was day nine. My brain throbbed with fashion after watching it day in and day out for almost a week and a half straight. I felt like I was in a deprivation tank, seeing, touching, and smelling nothing but clothes. I had tried varying the pace, occasionally worming my way backstage, huddled inside the mass of television crews that pushed past the groupies to ask the designer, what had inspired the magic? On one such adventure I found myself within spitting distance of Claude Montana. The Paris designer had been hot in the 1980s. Space-age chic, I think he had been known for. I had forgotten about him, but, standing close to him, I could see where he had gotten his ideas. He definitely looked as if he was from another planet. He had dyed blonde hair that looked like a toupee covering one eye. His skin was shockingly red and leprous. He spoke with a lisp. At one point, I thought I saw him drool. To me, he was utterly repellent.

A videographer from Montreal recognized me from the press bus that had taken us from the Louvre to some of the shows staged in various sites across Paris, the Moulin Rouge and Trocadéro among them. "He murdered his model wife, you know, pushed her out the apartment window. This show is his comeback," he whispered in my ear.

"From prison?" I gasped, perhaps a little too loudly. A press attaché was soon at my elbow, ushering me away.

I had taken the press bus again that day. The afternoon show, to which I had a real sit-down invitation, was being held at the Grand Palais, the ornate glass-roofed exhibition hall located near the Place de la Concorde. There was another interminable wait for the show to begin. None of the shows ever started on time, and this one was no exception. It was a brilliant sun-soaked afternoon. To pass the time, I stood outside under a plane tree, observing the carved figure of Apollo sitting on top of a corner of the belle-époque building. He was holding the reins of a chariot pulled by galloping horses—a figure of arresting beauty. I turned to look at the Seine, sparkling in the distance. The grass was green despite the season. Around me were bushes shaped to resemble full-skirted evening gowns. It was the first time during the entire trip that I had stopped to admire the external loveliness of Paris. And it was lovely. Breathtaking, in fact. Even the buildings seemed to shine. I thought I would weep. Why had I been feeling like a trespasser? The gifts of Paris were for the taking—why had I lost sight of that? I felt a surge of happiness. I wanted to call someone and shout the news. I was in Paris, and Paris was beautiful. But who would I call? Canada was just a dial tone away, I thought, and pressed my wafer-thin cell phone to my ear.

How life had changed since my first trip to Paris twenty-two years earlier. Was it already that long ago? Making a call home used to be so arduous. I had had to line up for hours in a post office for a long-distance line to open up. Paris once seemed far away from home, but now there was so much of North America in it. Even some of the PR people who gave me a hard time were from my side of the Atlantic. Paris had joined the global village, and I didn't know if I liked that. I looked at the phone in my hand. I thought to call my mother. It would be easy to do; she didn't know I was in Paris. I had deliberately not told her. That's how much things had changed between us. I punched in the code for Canada and with a start, recalled the tirades. I remembered how dejected she made me feel. I stopped myself—it wasn't worth the risk. One false word and she would ruin the moment. It was no longer enough just to travel far to get away from her. I had to get her out of my heart, out of my mind. Be disciplined. I wished I could stop thinking of her, wished I didn't care. I flipped the phone shut.

I continued to wait for the fashion show to begin, but then a show of sorts erupted around me. The Japanese. They had taken out their cameras and were raucously photographing everything around them. I had spent the week watching them. They were a formidable group of fashion victims and players who moved in packs as they hunted down the latest look for their fellow consumers in Japan. I couldn't comprehend where they got their money. They were the only ones who arrived at the shows conspicuously toting shopping bags from Louis Vuitton and Chanel. They actually bought the big-ticket items. They didn't line up for the freebies. They didn't have to. They were filthy rich.

They swarmed unsuspecting pedestrians who were passing alongside the Grand Palais, and then bowed and giggled behind hands held tightly to mouths, as if revealing their fangs would constitute an offense. They had been acting this way all week, and with this ersatz show of modesty appeared to stand apart from the flashy vulgarity of the fashion shows where everything, quite literally, had been hanging out. And yet of all the nationalities at the Paris fashion shows, the Japanese seemed the most besotted by all the flash and trash. They wanted it for themselves, as if it were some kind of forbidden fruit. They squealed the loudest when rock chanteuse Gwen Stefani took her front-row seat at Christian Dior. They chased Hollywood celebrity Renée Zellweger around the runway at Balenciaga, begging her for a portrait. It was shameless idol worship, and they showed no restraint. They seemed single-handedly to feed the incongruous relationship that lately had been developing between high French fashion and middlebrow Western culture. They were so hungry for anything pop culture that a few of them were suddenly swarming me, demanding a photograph. Having been ignored all week, I felt flattered.

"What you wearing?" a young Japanese woman asked of me. She seemed to be a reporter. She had a notebook and a pen in hand. A cameraman stood behind her, clicking away. I was having what in fashionspeak was known as a moment.

"Ka-na-da," I shouted, looking at the lens from over one shoulder, a wave of nationalism coloring my cheeks. "To-ron-to." The scribe with the Mickey Mouse knapsack recorded my every word. She bowed. I bowed back. I would be famous in Osaka.

After the show at the Grand Palais, something forgettable by Karl Lagerfeld, the madness continued back at the Louvre, where again I took to watching the Japanese. I had read about a street in Tokyo where the young pay homage to Western pop stars, dressing up like them in full costume. I had marvelled at the photographs of wannabe Madonnas, wannabe Elvises. At the Paris fashion shows I was surprised to find among the Japanese a wannabe Anna Wintour, the editor-in-chief of American *Vogue*, nicknamed Nuclear Wintour for her reportedly devastating management style. The real Anna Wintour routinely sat Nero-like still in the front row of all the important shows, shielded behind large black sunglasses that had everyone guessing as to her reactions. The Tokyo Wintour often sat across from her on the other side of the catwalk, also in the front row, with her idol's look down pat. She had the same inky bob, the same eyebrow-concealing fringe, the same wiry thinness, and the same inscrutable smile. It must have unnerved the real Wintour to see herself parodied so accurately, and by a woman of some prominence. She was said to head a leading fashion magazine in Japan. Was imitation the best flattery? I found it instead rather creepy, and yet she intrigued me. I decided that day to shadow her. I had nothing else to do. I had no more invitations.

I was hot on her trail as soon as the crowd that had come to see the latest offering by the house of Paco Rabanne had disgorged onto the Rue de Rivoli. I hadn't a clue where she was going. But I saw that she was clutching a large black invitation and was walking toward the Carrousel entrance of the Louvre, where a throng had already gathered outside. There was an unmistakable smell of excitement in the air. I could tell that the scent led to a killer collection. But what was it? I pushed in close to my Asian ally. I had in mind an image of the Tokyo subway, where professional people-pushers squeezed people like sardines into cars. I thought she wouldn't mind me sticking to her coat. It was part of her culture. When Tokyo Wintour peered at me from over the upturned collar of her mink, her eyes hard behind her own dark sunglasses, I smiled at her. I pretended nothing was the matter. I towered above her. But she was the fashion behemoth and I the parasite on her back, getting close, closer, closest to something that seemed red hot. Fashion incarnate.

The Paris shows, the exclusive ones anyway, were protected by big burly bodyguards, who made sure that the wrong people didn't get in. This show was no exception. Two commandos formed a muscle barrier at the entrance. They were ruthless about eyeballing people's invitations. There were shouts of anger and outrage. And then I heard the words Viktor & Rolf. I was at Viktor & Rolf? No wonder the crowd was going wild. This was the show no one could get into. And yet my girl had a ticket.

I was now practically on top of Tokyo Wintour. I couldn't squeeze left. I couldn't squeeze right. I felt the crowd tight behind me, pushing forward as if to break down the ancient walls of the palace itself. It moved like a collective breath, in and out. Soon I was within reach of the door. Tokyo Wintour had shown her invitation. I tried to hold onto her sleeve as she breezed in, but she shook me off. One of the bodyguards looked at me, expectantly. I made like I had the invitation somewhere in my Made in Canada purse. I fumbled, stalling for time. I wondered what to do. I was now so close to the entrance. I felt there was no turning back, and besides, I would likely get killed, trampled on by a stampede of Christian Louboutins, no less.

The guard was now glaring at me, as if reading my mind. I had been thinking of ducking under his large fore-arm and running. And then I remembered the wolves at the Alexander McQueen show held earlier in the week at the Conciergerie. The feral beasts had been tethered to high-stepping models who pulled them along the catwalk on long chains. The animals tried to cower, terrified by the flashing lights of the photographers. When applause broke out, one of the wolves howled. Yes, fashion can be cruel, and fur was back with a vengeance that season. McQueen had made that trend palpably real. I worried that in Paris there could be more animals at the shows, and they'd send them snarling after me. And so I hesitated. Just then, as luck would have it, it started to rain, a sudden downpour. The crowd roared its displeasure. Suddenly there was a frantic push forward. I had to steady my fishnet-stockinged legs because I could feel myself being lifted by the maniacal energy of the mob. They wanted in, and out of the rain.

"*Il pleut,*" I said, absentmindedly, unaware that anyone was listening.

"But *Madame*," said the burly guard, regarding me with a bemused look on his face, "it always rains in Paris."

The crowd pushed harder and harder. We were like a battering ram. And then I was airborne. But still I had my wits about me. Instead of settling back on my feet, I fell forward and onto my stomach, just beyond the reach of Hercules, who was busily fending off an invading horde of fashion barbarians. I was in battle position and I shimmied forward, crawling under cover into enemy lines. A fight erupted behind me. I could hear expletives and the sickening thud of flesh on flesh. I had made it, I thought. And then to my horror I saw another line of security guards inside the building. Wow. This was some hot show. I told myself not to look at them. They were big and black, and they could probably crush me beneath their combat boots. I adopted the hauteur of the Paris fashionista. I made like I owned the joint. Fashion is all about appearances, remember. I walked disdainfully past them. Lucky for me, at that moment another interloper, obviously not as smooth, had gotten himself caught between their paws. It was my chance to slip by undetected, and I did, with my heart pounding.

I thought that the hounds (human and otherwise) might still come after me, and so was careful not to look too conspicuous, and not too cowardly, either. This fashion business was a fine art. I skulked toward a dark corner and bumped right into the fashion reporter from *The Toronto Star*. Our newspapers were supposed to be rivals. He had been keeping his distance from me the entire trip. But when he saw me, he practically fell into my arms. "Omigod," he said. "I am *soooo* embarrassed. I sneaked in, and I am not one to sneak into any place where I am not invited, but this is supposed to be a shit-kicking show and ..." I told him to relax, that I had sneaked in, too. He laughed. When the lights finally went down for the start of the Viktor & Rolf show, he stayed by my side *"en standing"* (we didn't dare try to rush an empty seat) and allowed me to hold onto his arm so that I could raise myself up on tiptoe to see the extravaganza unfolding on the runway.

That was the show to have stormed. It was magnificent, from start to finish. If what Balzac wrote is true, that dress is the expression of society, then what I saw at Viktor & Rolf suggested a communal need for escape from the ordinary, for transformation and absolution through an exaggerated means of scale. Called Black Hole, the collection of "conceptually glamorous" clothes, to quote the program handout, was both black and oversized, with blouses featuring shoulders that puffed out grotesquely like giant soufflés and dresses with bustles cut like enormous pincushions. Viktor & Rolf interpreted the mutton sleeve almost literally. The emaciated models wearing them looked like overfed creatures, freaks of their own flocks. Necklines riffed on a theme of the Elizabethan ruff. The clothes steamrollered down the runway in strict silence. Only the sound of jaws dropping at the sight of such a novel presentation could be heard.

Augmenting the performance-art aspect of the show was the fact that the faces of the models were painted completely black. The thick inky mask of makeup highlighted the principal hue of the collection itself. Later some American fashion journalists, perhaps sensitive to their country's slave-trading past, said in print that the Viktor & Rolf show was in poor taste. They believed that the blackened faces were a comment on minstrelsy. But I thought that the blackening was about eliminating the personality of the wearer to draw increased attention to the clothes, in particular the heft of their silhouette. The distortion of human scale suggested to me a promise of endless possibilities, while black implied wiping the slate clean. It was the beginning of the new millennium. Over the past year, people around the world had been venting their doomsday fears in the media. Black was also a funereal color. Were the designers, a Dutch duo with a background in visual art and theater, also lending expression to the inevitability of death? And yet the stateliness of the procession, the air of quiet dignity, not to mention the impeccable tailoring, made me feel uplifted by the clothes, as if they were acts of faith.

Black represented the end and the beginning of all things. The gargantuan dimensions of the clothes suggested something otherworldly, something bigger than me and this whole crazy Paris scene. I left Viktor & Rolf finally knowing my theme.

I had unearthed *the* trend of the season, and it was black. All the colors I had seen over the past week and a half had, in the recesses of my exhausted brain, bled into one dark-as-night hue. There had been black at Chanel and at Yves Saint Laurent, at Issey Miyake and Comme des Garçons. It was a rich metaphor to play with, and I found that I could apply it to many ideas that I had had about the collections in general. Black was night. Black was sin. Black was the obliteration of all rules that had previously dictated what constituted fashionable dressing. Black was mystery. Black veils suggested piety. Black leather made you think of kinky sex. I thought of the French obsession with film noir. There had been gangster looks on the runway and Mafia molls in the audience. Quentin Tarantino, the postmodern American cinéaste, was then a popular topic in French intellectual circles, discussed also in the Paris newspapers. His film *Reservoir Dogs*, in which the entire male cast was dressed in black, was then being rereleased in France. I drew a connection between his latest movie, *Pulp Fiction*, a noir-ish brew of a mixed-metaphor film, and the mixed messages offered up by the Paris shows. In the end I called the Paris collections for fall 2001 "Pulp Fashion."

I thought it clever at the time. But after my laptop crashed in the middle of the night following a power outage, and I had to frantically rewrite the article on the backs of napkins in a late-night brasserie located next to my hotel, fearing I would forget what I had just said, I felt vanquished by my own inability to rise to the occasion. Paris fashion, for all the tomfoolery of the last ten days, was still a kind of ideal. It symbolized the unrivalled artifice of Paris, what had long held me in thrall. I had wanted to do it justice. But I felt frustrated by my efforts. Once more Paris made me feel that I didn't quite reach the mark, that I wasn't good enough, that I needed to try harder. I worried that I hadn't adequately described Paris fashion as a mirror of life's vacillating elements, its essentially changing nature. I felt disappointed in myself.

After I rewrote and emailed my story at about four in the morning Paris time, I collapsed into my bed, and fell into a fitful sleep. I dreamed that the wolves had found me hiding under a silk-wrapped chair at one of the by-invitation-only shows. A bodyguard dressed like a member of the gestapo, head to toe in Hugo Boss, hauled me out by the scruff of my neck. I would be publicly punished, forced to walk the runway and kiss Claude Montana fully on his liver-colored lips. I did so, and then he slapped me, calling me an idiot. "Dunt you know anysing?" he shouted in accented English. "It goes like zis!" And then he shoved his tongue down my throat, almost suffocating me.

I woke with a start, thinking that I needed to get out of Paris before I, too, toppled out a window. Because I had filed my story, I didn't feel a need to go to any more shows. I had two days left before I returned to Toronto. I thought I would go shopping, hunt down some of those bewitching ensembles I had seen on the runway. Most wouldn't be in the stores until the fall. But I had had a sneak preview of what would be "in," and I thought I could find some pieces that would enable me to replicate some of the styles for myself on the cheap. I was quickly discouraged. I had been living in such a make-believe world these past ten days that I had lost sight of the fact that all this so-called interpretive chic actually cost a fortune to create and maintain. In Paris a ruched dress such as I saw on the runway at Cacharel cost upwards of $3,000. I was beginning to think that I had written the wrong article. I had become seduced by the image of French fashion and hadn't noted how out of touch it was with the reality of most women's lives. Who wears the million-dollar jewel-encrusted jeans I saw on the runway, anyway? A distributor told me they were popular among princesses and other consorts living in the oil-rich Arab countries. I swallowed hard. I was no princess, but at the Paris shows I had lived the illusion. It was time to crash back down to earth.

And so I made the dreaded call to Toronto, the one in which I would have to supplicate myself before a stiff-backed editor on the other end of the line. I imagined the lecture awaiting me, reminding me that so much money had been spent on me and that I hadn't delivered. She would tell me that Paris fashion was a "soft" story, beneath her contempt, really. She would tell me to rewrite it all, find a new angle, and that upon my return I would be named the radio reporter, doomed to cover the CBC. While she no doubt would be shouting at me, I'd be scrupulous in not mentioning that the weather in Paris had been uncharacteristically delightful, with freshly blossomed flowers sprouting everywhere. I would not talk about the champagne, either. Or the beauty treatments, and the free stuff.

But such is the self-delusory world of the writer. You think you have been good, and then an editor tells you have been bad. You think you have been bad, and then an editor tells you, surprise, not only have you been good, but great, worthy of the expense of sending you to Paris.

That was what, to my astonishment, I heard when I called Toronto. I got praise, genuine acclaim. My usual editor had come down with the flu, so hadn't been around to handle my copy when it came in. Another editor, a man with no claims on the fashion beat, had that day taken her place. He was a transplanted Brit and he loved what I wrote. He told me that colleagues had jostled with each other to read my copy before it went to press. "It was that good." He laughed. "I've never had so much fun reading fashion before. Well done. You captured Paris."

He would have no idea what his words meant to me. He had lifted me out of my slump—that was the immediate effect his praise had on me. But more significantly, he made me feel that I had somehow accomplished a long-held goal about Paris. I had fathomed its depths.

I dressed in my finery that day and took a walk through the Jardin du Luxembourg. Those who have experienced Paris have the advantage over those who haven't. We are the ones who have glimpsed a little bit of heaven, down here on earth.

EIGHT

Mother

· 2007 ·

I TOOK MY two children for an impromptu visit to Paris in the soggy weeks preceding Christmas 2007. It was supposed to be a miniholiday, just the three of us, with a little reporting on the side. I was now *The Globe and Mail*'s general assignment reporter for the new weekly Toronto section, but still occasionally contributed to other parts of the paper—style, travel, real estate, and life. I lost the fashion beat after being absent from work for an extended period following the birth of my daughter in 2003. A life-threatening illness crippled me when she was just six months old. It was something totally befuddling and unpredictable, and frustrating to all the experts. I couldn't walk or bathe myself, let alone hold or nurse my newborn.

My yearlong maternity leave stretched into a three-year disability leave, during which I was treated with a mighty arsenal of drugs that made me bloated, manic, out of control. While the medications didn't kill the disease, they subdued it to the point that in January 2006 I was able to walk, on my own steam, back into my workplace, only to discover I had been reassigned.

But work was still allowing me to return to Paris. This time I was in the city to research a couple of travel articles, focused on kids and the City of Light. A good fit, or not? I wasn't sure what the outcome would be. I had only once before been in Paris with children—and they had belonged to other people. That was a long time ago, and my memory was of a city where children were mostly not seen or heard, confined as they were to city parks whose iron gates were locked at night, forbidding fun of the family variety after dark. True, the traffic in Paris was too dangerous for children to play unsupervised out on narrow cobblestone streets. And so I understood the necessity of keeping them sequestered within leafy oases boasting pony rides, puppet shows, or, as is the case at the Parc Zoologique just outside Paris at Vincennes, flocks of pink flamingoes. But beyond those confines? Could Paris, city of lovers, work its magic also on the school-age set? The journalist in me wanted to find out. But the mother in me harbored a deeper purpose. I wanted to expose my offspring early to the city that had for so long played inside the shelter of my own imagination. Perhaps I wanted them to get to know me better so that after I was dead and buried and they looked back at their life with me, they wouldn't focus on the mistakes but remember the beautiful obsession I had wanted to share with them, in hopes of firing their own imaginations to face the future.

But in getting them to dream with me, I might have overstepped myself. I hadn't considered the consequences of blithely getting my children to play truant. My son's grade 3 teacher retaliated by loading us down with a bagful of math homework ("so he won't fall behind," she had said firmly) to be completed by the time we returned to Toronto eight days later. I say "we" because I was the one who had to organize the morning study sessions and know the right answer from the wrong answer in order to help my eight-year-old get through the work.

It was geometry, which I hadn't contemplated in years, and in a way it was ironic that we had brought it with us to Paris, the city where several centuries earlier Descartes had formulated a system of knowing the world based on geometric principles. Soon after arriving there, my brain was swimming with questions regarding the relative position of figures of varying shapes, sizes, and spatiality in relation to others. It was hard going; math has never been my strong suit. It was exact. My thinking seemed to be more all over the place. It also reminded me of my short-comings as a mother, of how much I had become like the one I used to come to Paris to escape. Impatient, agitated, a yeller. Like at that moment, tapping a finger on the textbook page explaining how the shortest distance between two points is a straight line. I shouted at my son to repeat the rule back to me. We'd gone over it a zillion times, but still he wasn't getting it. "Focus!" I hammered. He looked to be daydreaming, his green-blue eyes fixed on a spot beyond the window. I shouldn't have blamed him.

Our room was located on the 17th floor of a residential building in the 15th Arrondissement, a suburban neighborhood close to parks and a supermarket. I hadn't wanted to chase tots up spiralling staircases in a centuries-old hotel—charming in another life, but utterly impractical now. So on this trip I had opted for a kitchenette suite in an apartment-hotel, a relatively new concept for Paris, and a sign that the city was warming to the idea of family travel. It was a spacious corner unit, with windows for walls and sweeping views of the city, stretching from the undulating Seine in the east to the dome of the Panthéon in the west. Immediately before us loomed the Eiffel Tower, global icon of Paris. Now that I had geometry on the brain, I noted that it was a large three-dimensional column with a square base, a mathematically balanced structure. Bronze in color. A thing of rare beauty. My son called it the rocket ship, observing that its steel-clad nose butted the air as if at any moment it might burst through the clouds and take flight, high above Paris.

Beyond, looking like a milky mirage upon the hill, was Sacré-Cœur, reminding me of my husband, whom I had left behind. He was a professor now and he couldn't skip class. But not bringing him had been a mistake, I told myself. He was the good cop; I was the scolder-in-chief.

My four-year-old daughter was used to it. While I ranted at my son she sat quietly at my feet, drawing with her crayons a smiling, dark-haired lady with a heart on her dress and a rainbow for a hat. "It's you, mama," she smiled, holding up the picture for me to admire. Lovely. Heart-breaking, really.

I stood up and looked out the window at Paris, my mood connecting with the silt-brown gush of the river. Trees lined the banks of the Seine, their leaves still green, despite it being the first day of December. I could see flowers in bloom on the rooftop gardens of surrounding apartment buildings. I could see people watching television. People having lunch. A man in a red scarf walked a dog on a leash in the park below, where children in colorful hats used sticks to trace their own made-up shapes in the mud.

I thought of the day before, our first day in Paris together, and how I had made us withstand the urge to sleep after our transatlantic flight. Maybe we were all still just very tired. I had taken them first to the grocery store, where we bought frozen pizza, chocolate milk, and candied chestnuts, *marrons glacés,* the dessert that always said Paris to me. After, we walked the short distance from our hotel on Rue du Théâtre to the quay near the Eiffel Tower, where we boarded a Bateau Mouche. I thought a boat ride down the Seine would be a good way to give them a feel for the city without them having to walk. We sat on the open deck, the weather that first day being full of sunshine. They were too young to heed the boat's prerecorded commentary illuminating the history of Paris through some of the monuments edging the Seine. As we chugged along under the city's bridges, they called out nonsense words to hear them echo back, as they laughed uproariously.

My daughter eventually nodded off, dropping like a stone into sleep, the way children will suddenly do. Her daisylike head wilted onto the boat's railing. I had to hold on to her for fear she'd topple into the river. When the ride came to a stop, I revived her with an invitation to ride the carousel near the Jardin du Trocadéro, close to the riverbank. With her brother, she whirled round and round on a painted horse, waving at me each time she passed me by. I bought them crêpes smeared with Nutella at the nearby concession booth. A pair of gypsy women attired in head kerchiefs and thick layers of colorful skirts worked the crowd. In their hennaed hands they held a stack of index cards. I hadn't paid attention until one of them shoved a card under my nose, compelling me to read. "I am sick, with six children to feed. Please help." I was halfway through the typewritten plea when I realized I'd bitten the bait. I saw her signal to her cohort. She had caught one.

An unsuspecting *étrangère* with more money than brains. They probably just wanted my handbag. But I glanced fearfully at my children, stuffing themselves, their little pale faces smeared with chocolate, worried the gypsies would snatch them instead. I rushed over to pull them close to my body, a nervous mother hen.

Turning now to my son, still gazing out the window, I said, with a softer voice this time, that if he couldn't tell me by the count of three how far a straight line between two points could reach, that was it. No swimming pool. "Um." One. "Ah." Two. "Indefinitely!" Three. Saved by the bell.

There was a swimming pool in the bowels of the building. I herded the kids out into the hallway, their bathing suits already under their clothes, and pushed the elevator button. It didn't ding. It spoke. *"La porte est ouverte,"* announced a discombobulated but dewy-sounding female voice as the door opened. *"La porte est fermée,"* it acknowledged as the door closed. *"Descendez,"* continued the voice, assuredly, when the high-tech lift plummeted, taking us two floors below the reception area to the subterranean spa. That's what I need, I thought as the kids stood spellbound inside the polished-chrome box. Computerized emotion. Everything regulated. Destination defined.

The doors opened again, and my kids ran to jam their things into a wall of lockers. I watched as they, *mes enfants*, scurried to the pool's edge: their elegantly proportioned limbs, their effortlessly straight backs, pliant as plasticine, the funny way they went forward on tiptoe, elbows fused to ribs, sucking on their fingers from excitement, and the goose-pimpling cold. They danced the tarantella as they peered deliriously into the blue, daring each other. "You go! No, you!" Both then leapt in fearlessly at the same time, smiling as they sank. "I can touch the bottom," yelped my son, bubbling back up to the surface. "Can you?" I murmured, "Can you, really? Clever boy."

The swim had tired us out—it was already ten o'clock at night—and once back upstairs in our ultramodern hotel room, upholstered in sapphire blue and pumpkin orange, I dressed my twosome in their pajamas and got them straight under the starched white sheets. I read them a story, something with a nativity theme given the season, and before turning off the lights sat with them to look out the window at the Eiffel Tower. It was lit up like a Christmas tree, sparkling and flashing in the velvety darkness. Paris in the sky with diamonds. Inside the tower's straddled legs were large boxlike elevators. We watched them go down, their steady rhythm making us all rather sleepy. I reached to turn off the bedside light and promised the children that we'd go up ourselves. They asked me what we'd find. I told them I couldn't say, exactly. In all my years coming to Paris, I had only ever admired this ur-symbol of the city from afar, never venturing up. This was because I had heard that it typically took hours of waiting in line to ride to the top, and that had seemed a waste of time to me. I also hadn't thought that looking out over Paris from above would serve me better than exploring it on foot below, preferring serendipitous discoveries of the city's treasures and mysteries to some prescribed touristy journey. But what was that to kids? They wanted the destination, not the journey. They wanted to go straight to the top. I wasn't going to deny them that pleasure, so I promised them, yes, we would ride the Eiffel Tower.

But the next day we woke to rain and bruised skies. Not good for riding to the top of Paris, I said to their chorus of moans. They clamored for a return to the swimming pool, which I vetoed, wanting to hold it in reserve as a treat for good behavior. I bundled them up, and we went outside, where the trees sighed and dropped the last of the summer's leaves into the gutter. But I wanted this to be a day unlike the days before. A day when I wouldn't yell. A day I would just try to enjoy for itself, I thought, as I marched the kids down the bustling Avenue Émile Zola, which was overhung with Christmas lights shaped like chandeliers, sparkling despite the downpour. I gave each child a coin and told them what to say in French to buy one of the cookies heaped delectably in a shop window. My daughter was game, but my son grew tongue-tied. Tears welled in his eyes. He said he was afraid of making a mistake, which I said was ridiculous, before realizing that in Paris I often had the same fear. He was the spitting image of my husband; everyone said so. A narrow face with rosebud lips and vaulted eyebrows. But at that moment I realized he was more like me. When we had been in the grocery store on the first day, I had brusquely hushed them when they went about chattering loudly in the aisles, playing sport with the live lobsters holed up in a much-too-small aquarium in the seafood section. "Stop speaking English!" I had blurted, feeling my foreignness in that store like a brand on my frowning forehead. "But we speak English!" wailed my daughter. I told her to shut up altogether, then. I was so embarrassed by my own imagined sense of inferiority among the French that I lashed out, hurting my own children. I left the store loaded down with plastic shopping bags, my children skipping gaily ahead, wondering, when in Paris would I ever relax?

The French tourist office had organized a lunch for us at Chez Clément, on the Champs-Élysées, its contribution to my story about children in Paris. I suppose the idea was to make sure I made note that the city of gastronomic adventure was inclusive of finicky palates of all ages. In any event I was glad for the free meal and a glimpse into an establishment that definitely would have eluded me in my life before kids. The decor consisted of old pots and pans hanging from the rafters, gingham curtains, and brightly painted flowerpots. The restaurant was large and spread out over two floors. Adults sat at most of the tables, it being Paris at noon, the time when everyone in the city, it seemed, stopped for lunch. We were shepherded downstairs, making me think that little had changed in Paris where children and dining was concerned. But there I spied whimsical furnishings in the form of high chairs made out of old grandfather clocks. The tight-lipped maître d' handed us three large menus, obviously assuming the children could read, and read French. For which I didn't want to chastise him, glad to think someone else recognized them as budding prodigies. The menu offered typical bistro fare—poached salmon, roast chicken, crème brûlée. There was also a children's menu, offering simply a main dish, a dessert, and a drink. But it was recommended I select from the elaborate five-course prix fixe menu, which I did, being a guest. My ravenous children ate steadily through the bread and the beef, but they turned their noses up at the liver pâté and the *soupe à l'oignon* that came with their meals. They claimed suddenly to be full and repeatedly ran out of their brightly painted chairs to the bathroom, leaving me to finish their chocolate ice creams. The maître d', whom I thought had been barely tolerating us, appeared smiling at meal's end with yo-yos, which he gave to each child. My son's was royal-blue, my daughter's pink. They sat transfixed as this suddenly jolly man showed them tricks like how to rock the cradle and walk the dog. *"Merci,"* said my son, trying out some French. *"Merci,"* said my daughter. Instant cosmopolitans.

They played with their new toys as we exited the restaurant to merge with the strolling afternoon crowds out on the avenue. Rolling them up, rolling them down. They were too absorbed with their playthings to care that flowers were freakishly in blossom near the Grand Palais, or that the high-heel ankle boots on the leggy women ambling with their packages seemed to be the latest Paris fashion. I took in every detail. The fancy car dealerships. The purple awnings etched in gold. Club Med and Guerlain, internationally recognized French brands. The international banks, the perfumed boutiques, the huzzah. A world of wanting and getting, singing its own praises. I enjoyed observing the commercial hubbub, not feeling at all shut out. Been there, Done that, Time to move on.

The children were unaware, but I had planned for our walk down the Champs-Élysées to end at the Place de la Concorde, where there was a giant Ferris wheel, a leftover from the city's millennium celebrations seven years earlier. When they finally saw it, their eyes popped, and they did a little jig, asking me, please, oh please, could we take a ride.

We lined up to buy our tickets, and when it was our turn to board the Roue de Paris, a worker with large arms hoisted my kids into one of the cars before offering me a hand to climb in myself. He clicked the bar shut, a slender piece of steel, and suddenly off we flew, fast into the air. I felt the jolt of liftoff and slid wildly, threatening to crush my children laughing loudly next to me. With a start I realized that there were no safety belts, no barriers other than that puny bar which I gripped, my knuckles turning white. In Canada this would never have been allowed! A lawsuit waiting to happen. But too late. "Hold on!" I screamed as I felt the mighty wheel turning. "Whatever you do, don't fall off!"

We went around and around, faster and faster. We sailed high above the treetops and floated momentarily in the air when the car stopped to allow others on and off on the ground far below. The wheel turned again, and we felt ourselves plummeting. I screamed. I was terrified, but giddy at the same time, whirling high above the treetops of Paris. The city looked like a giant jigsaw puzzle whose myriad pieces were the thousands of buildings squeezed tightly together to form a magnificent whole. With one hand I fumbled to open the lens cap on the camera hanging around my neck. It was such an extraordinary perspective. The copper rooftops. The snaking Seine and, directly below, the obelisk, the baroque fountains, and the Jardin des Tuileries with its manicured hedges and linear columns and motley groups of people sitting and reading and kissing and looking just fine amid the alleyways of artfully pruned trees—human nature and Mother Nature having found their life of harmony. The ground was the color of churned-up sand from all the people who had walked there before, over the centuries. But I didn't take a picture of that. I took a picture of my children. Their faces were open and gleeful, their Chiclet teeth blazing white as the wind wrought havoc through their hair.

When I got off, I felt the ground push up under me with a thump. My legs wobbly, I turned into the gardens, corralling the children to come with me. I headed toward some green metal chairs that encircled a large basin nestled in between the Jeu de Paume (the former royal tennis courts) and the Orangerie museum. I needed to catch my breath. As I sat, the children ran after some ducks, making them scud across the surface of the water. The sun was setting, the sky mottled orange and pink. It looked like a Pointillist painting made of an infinite number of colored dots. We walked only a few steps away and then saw, close to the Rue de Rivoli, a playground hidden beneath the boxwood trees. There was a gate, of course. But it was unlocked. I pushed it open, and the children shot inside, finding a series of large-scale spinning tops that they pushed and then jumped onto, blurring as they rapidly turned. As if the day hadn't already been dizzying enough.

From there we moved on, finding next giant red boxes on bouncy coils that the children rode like buckaroos. At the center of this serendipitous playground fantasy land was a large steel column, a kind of modern-day maypole, but dangling knotted lengths of rope instead of colored ribbon. The children each grabbed hold of a length and danced about, weaving them into a complex pattern of braids. After they tired of that game, they zigzagged through a maze of knee-high hedges before stumbling upon an enclosure where, buried in the ground, was a series of trampolines, inviting kids to get airborne on their own steam. It was all wondrously fantastic.

I had been to Paris over so many years, but never knew such small-fry pleasures existed inside its famous gardens. It wasn't a part of the Tuileries that was advertised. I supposed you just had to know where to go, and to do that, you had to be looking at Paris through a child's eyes, as a place of hidden delights. I paid two euros to a lady, the keeper of the trampolines, who approached me with an outstretched palm. She instantly took charge. In a singsong voice she told the children to take off their boots, which they did after I translated her instructions. It was after dusk, and at that time of the day only one other child was playing on the trampolines, a dainty thing in a pompom hat whose lamblike whiteness matched the color of her gloves. My children bounced boldly past her like kangaroos. They tumbled wildly, trying out a variety of airborne maneuvers. Running, somersaulting, twirling. The little Parisian girl stared as she watched brother and sister collide with each other to fall flat on their faces. As soon as they were down, they bounced back up again.

Their paid time was up. They put their boots back on and raced ahead. They said they heard music. I listened. A delicate tendril of sound. I followed behind and within seconds found myself standing, dazzled, in front of a merry-go-round inscribed with a gilt-edged "Carrousel la Belle Époque." It was covered with a fading rose motif and strings of colored bulbs. It looked ancient, an old beauty, but I had never noticed it before. The ride was already turning by the time we reached it, but no one was on it. My children stood beside it, admiring the hand-carved steeds with long flowing horsehair for tails. I saw a booth with a man inside, dark-skinned with a stiff, grizzled mustache. He sat alone behind a grille, facing the spectacle of enchantment. I approached to buy two tickets. The box behind him was dark. He quietly took my money, then activated a lever that made the ride come to a halt. The children clambered on, hauling themselves into sherbet-colored saddles with real leather reins. "I'm a professional cowgirl," shouted my daughter as the ride started up again. My son remained quiet, with a dreamy look on his face. "Good horsey," he said, patting his horse as if it were alive. "Good horsey."

The ticket man called out to me. He asked where I was from. He had a brother in Toronto, he said after I answered, and then paused, looking suddenly melancholy. He said his brother drove a taxi, in a faraway place that was very cold. He said he hadn't seen him in years. *"Il y a longtemps,"* he shrugged. I didn't know what to say, so together we looked at the merry-go-round transporting my children inside their dream worlds. The ride slowed to a finish, the music dying. The man looked at me, his eyelids beating quickly over his sad-looking eyes. He hit the lever to start the ride up again, saying the next spin was on the house. I was beginning to think that maybe Paris was for children after all. Here was an angle I hadn't considered before. In this unexpected act of empathy, I could see that what made Paris endlessly intriguing to me, and never the same city twice, were the people who inhabited it. Sure, the city was a treasure trove of things, captivatingly beautiful: statuary, paintings, magnificent architecture, and enchanting parks. So often on my travels to the city I had been overwhelmed by its surface grandeur, thinking Paris an ideal that I could scarcely live up to. But I was learning that beyond the gilded facade, Paris was a tight weave of interconnected stories, personal narratives engendered by chance encounters in a city where the only constant was change. In that way, Paris was like this painted carousel, spinning around and around in a multicolored blaze of lights. A city of endless possibilities, never quite grasped.

Suddenly it was dark, night falling like a curtain. It had also started to rain. I popped open my umbrella and pulled down my children's hats, zipping their coats up to their chins. The drizzle became a downpour as we walked up Rue de Castiglione, hugging the outsides of expensive jewelry boutiques to snatch whatever shelter we could. We forged on, through the Place Vendôme and on to the Rue de la Paix, in the direction of the Opéra. In the metro I had seen posters advertising the Christmas windows at the *grands magasins*, on Boulevard Haussmann. I would take them there as a treat. I asked if they could hang on, make the trek, as we'd be walking far. They nodded their heads.

A glow rose from behind the Palais Garnier. The department stores were festooned with lights, a Las Vegas blaze of electric color spelling out the words *Joyeux Noël* in large twinkling letters. Beckoning us. I took the children by the hand and led them across the rain-streaked boulevard, where a crowd had gathered in front of the Galeries Lafayette to see more than a thousand mechanical toys spinning through a winter wonderland made of crystal and mirrors. I gave them permission to squeeze through the wall of large-backed adults. Once through, they climbed onto wooden platforms erected outside on the sidewalk, enabling little ones a close-up view of the pageantry behind the store's billboard-sized windows. Pressing their noses up against the glass, they stood transfixed by a spectacle depicting a band of saxophone-playing panda bears backed by a choir of snowy owls, boisterously heralding the joy of the season. My children stood there a long while, oblivious to the cold, lit up by thousands of bulbs designed to look like a snowflake shower. Eventually they moved on to the next window, featuring a herd of guffawing reindeer, and then on to another, where a posse of windup polar bears swung on chandeliers or else pickaxed the floor of what otherwise looked like a respectable holiday party. It made the children laugh out loud, uproariously.

Watching them made me think of when I was small, standing in front of the Christmas windows at the Eaton's department store in downtown Toronto. The Canadian windows were rooted in the Victorian era, and I had thought them beautiful. They might have lacked the carnival-like whimsy of the Paris windows, but they were still all about weaving fantasy. These were windows that showed the world as tiny and perfect, where families ate together around a dollhouse-sized dining-room table topped with food and sang together, sharing intimate glances. A dream world preserved behind glass. My favorite had been the window devoted to Santa's toy shop, where mechanical bears clapped their cymbals, dolls in petticoats blew kisses, and silvery electric trains went round and round a familiar track.

Santa Claus didn't live in Paris. And the snow in the store's window was ersatz. But I realized I had something better when my daughter slipped her wet mittened hand into mine, pulling me to look at something that had caught her eye. It was a mise-en-scène, equal parts poetic and absurd, a Paris specialty, and it boasted a horde of penguins blowing bubbles into the stratosphere. My son was there, drunk on the illusion. The bubbles rose above the candy-floss landscape and didn't burst.

ON THIS TRIP I had wanted to revisit some of my old haunts along the Boulevard Saint-Germain, with its Latin Quarter side streets of Rue de Seine, Rue de Buci and Rue Saint-André des Arts. This is where I used to sit for hours, lingering over a coffee or a glass of wine, my chair on a *café terrasse* affording me a front-row seat to some of the world's best people-watching. I wanted to share the places I liked with my children, hoping that perhaps they would see what I found unique in Paris, a city whose old, narrow, and winding streets made it feel intimate and embracing. It was an illusion, of course, because Paris itself was hard to penetrate, remaining tantalizingly on the margins of my imagination as a city that teased but never lay itself down for conquest. Still, that boutique image of Paris resonated. It served as a bracing antidote to my own city, Toronto, created on a grid, and so cold and sprawling and impersonal by comparison. Paris was where I believed I could relish sensual pleasures as well as feed a craving for intellectual pursuits. It had suggested to me an opportunity for a more sophisticated standard of everyday living. I liked that in Paris I could walk into a bar with my kids and not be turned away, as I was in Toronto for cavalierly exposing minors to the horror of an aperitif-drinking mother. But that feeling of having my kids and a *kir* too was short-lived.

When I took my children to the Café de Flore, they complained about the cigarette smell. In Paris people still smoke, unlike in Canada. My kids loudly declared it disgusting and plugged their noses. I dragged them over to the Jardin du Luxembourg, thinking to stick to where the wild things roamed. There, my terrible twosome gleefully rode a pair of old donkeys and another antique carousel, where an old man handed them wooden sticks with which to pole a brass ring. We also visited the less-well-trodden Jardin des Plantes and watched the doe-eyed wallabies misting in the rain. The natural history museum was nearby, and we ducked inside the glass-roofed Grande Galerie de l'Évolution to escape the incessant downpour. There, beneath the skeleton of a giant blue whale suspended from the ceiling, we wandered among a prodigious array of animals, slaughtered then stuffed in the name of science: hippopotamuses, giraffes, lions, zebras, narwhals, mother elephants with their trumpeting young, and butterflies, some as big as stingrays. It made me queasy walking through it, a graveyard built in pursuit of knowledge. But the kids loved looking at the kaleidoscope of creatures parading silently across an imagined savanna land, and so I persevered, climbing the old wooden stairs to study my likeness in the face of an ape. The most curious exhibit, at least to my mind, was that of the stuffed royal rhino—once a pet of Louis xv, that had come from the menagerie at Versailles. The information sheet said that it was brought to Paris as an object of public education. I saw the little hairs on its back, the funny way the mouth pulled sideways below the horn. A smile, or a grimace. I couldn't tell which.

After having tasted this museum, filled with curiosities older than the French Revolution, I was emboldened to find others that children would also effortlessly find thrilling. These included the Paris Doll Museum, located close to the Centre Pompidou, and Le Grand Rex, an art deco cinema on the Boulevard Poissonnière, where we took a backstage tour through an old movie set and became the stars of our own spaghetti western. Afterward, the three of us went front of house where, once more needing to wait out the December rains, we sat in large plush red velvet seats and watched a first-run screening of a French film called *Le Renard et l'Enfant,* based on an old French fairy tale about a little girl and her pet fox, who lives in a wood. When she forces the animal to come live with her in her house it runs wild, breaking dishes and nearly dying when it leaps for freedom out a glass window. It was in French, and the children didn't comprehend a word. Yet they seemed visibly moved by this story about a love so strong it transcended all reason.

We took the metro to Saint-Paul, in the Marais, and walked down Rue Saint-Antoine, the main drag in medieval times, past a jumble of old buildings and narrow passageways that my kids were eager to run into. We were looking for Number 11 Rue Saint-Paul, where the words Académie de Magie were painted over the arched doorway. We had to climb down a steep flight of stairs to reach the entrance. There the children encountered a disembodied hand that reached out to them to give their own hands a shake. But they quickly let go when a painted head popped from inside the box, giving them a fright.

I bought our tickets and was told, *vite!* Hurry, the magic show was about to start. I rushed the children to take their places in the theater located down a narrow passageway, beneath a barrelled ceiling. The bleachers were full because of a school trip. Sylvain, as the man with a goatee introduced himself, took the tiny stage and, with a swirl of his satin cape, began his repertoire of tricks.

The first involved a deck of cards, with the diamonds increasing and decreasing in number each time he waved it, *un-deux-trois,* in front of his ample tummy. The next involved a piece of string that with a dramatic roll of the wrist, Sylvain the magician transformed into three smaller strings of equal length. All the children "oohed" and "aahed," mine included. They couldn't understand a word he was saying, but it didn't seem to matter.

I looked around us. We were sitting inside what seemed like an underground vault supported by elegant columns exploding upward into arches. Later, one of the magicians told me that we were in the cellar of a former royal palace. But when I got home and looked the museum up on the Internet, I read that it was actually the former home of the Marquis de Sade. In any event it seemed that tricks had been turning there for centuries.

After the show was over, we wandered the claustrophobic corridors stuffed with curiosities, carnival relics, and the former belongings of Jean Eugène Robert-Houdin, the French illusionist born in 1805, said to be the father of modern magic and to whom the museum was dedicated. There were secret boxes, false doors, an automated fortune-teller peering into a crystal ball, and a framed portrait of a dark-suited, bearded man that collapsed when I walked by, startling me.

My children were in a back room howling with laughter. I followed the delirious sound and found them in front of a wall of fun-house mirrors, the kind that distort the body, making it seem dwarfish, supertall, or grotesquely fat. I stood behind them and regarded myself, chopped off at the knees and dwarfed by half my normal size. "Mommy's a midget!" they squealed. "Mommy's a midget!"

Seeing how the mirror made multiples of them, I was reminded of how I had in a moment of weakness confided in my mother my desire to have many more children, even though time was quickly running out.

"You don't want that," she scowled. "Children get in the way. They destroy ambition. Cramp your style. You don't have a life of your own when you have children."

I realized then that she had regarded her own children that way. As a burden. And it was why she stayed away from my children, and rarely called. "Children get in the way." In the midst of all my inwardly swirling fury, a light had gone off. It hadn't been my fault that she was so distant, just as it wasn't my children's fault. It was her. It was how she viewed her world, distorted as it was. That's when I recognized that she would never change. And that I was on my own, raising my own children, my precious children, with little to guide me but a need to be different—to be not like her.

It was dusk when we left that museum's sleight-of-hand world. I dragged the children on a cook's tour of the district. The open courtyard of the 17th-century Hôtel de Sully. The arcade of Place des Vosges, where we stumbled upon a lineup of women and their children, patiently waiting to get inside a by-invitation-only designer children's clothing sale.

We pushed toward the Quai d'Orléans and stood on the bridge. The Seine sloshed under us, impetuous and dangerous. My daughter threw herself up the railing. "I want to see," she said. "I want to see!" "Get down from there," I shrieked. I thought she'd topple over the rail. My lashing tone had frightened her, and she started to cry. I knew the feeling and held her close.

My embrace cheered her in an instant, her mood shifting like a cloud passing in front of the sun. She skipped ahead to join her brother, who had turned to look at her, concerned.

On the Pont Saint-Louis, a beggar man was on the bridge, playing an accordion. He was fingering a distinctly French song, teeming with love and tender regret. The rain had stopped. The moon was in the sky, and Notre Dame loomed in the background, illuminated like a prayer. It felt like a perfect Paris moment, my daughter twirling to the music, the moonlight floating above the faultless roundness of my son's head, exposed to the elements. Paris had become my heart.

I rooted in my wallet for some change. I called the children over to me and told them to drop the money in the man's cap, lying open on the ground, shining from the rain. With rheumy eyes he looked at my kids, and he called out to them as they skipped way into the star-spangled night, *"Merci mon prince! Merci ma princesse!"*

WE WOKE THE next day to the rare sight of blazing sunshine. Finally, a day to go up the Eiffel Tower. The mighty triangle, as my daughter called it, having listened in on her brother's lessons. "No, a pyramid," he corrected her. I told them not to squabble and hurried them into their clothes, shoving into their hands prepackaged Belgian waffles that I nuked in the microwave in our stainless-steel kitchen. It was early, not yet eight o'clock. We could see that the tower's elevators weren't yet hauling tourists. I hoped to beat the crowds. We could walk there, it was so close.

We exited Rue du Théâtre and climbed up the steps on the Quai de Grenelle, scooting alongside the Seine on a raised bed with a pedestrian walkway. We passed the barges on the river, and also the Stade Émile-Anthoine, where a soccer game was already underway. Everyone seemed to be taking advantage of the freakishly good weather. People walked with their coats tied around their waists. Shopkeepers smilingly bid us *bonjour!* as we stepped smartly past their just-swept doorways, the smell of garlic hanging heavily in the air. Even the grounds surrounding the tower on the Champ de Mars seemed to possess an unnatural brightness that day. The grass was emerald-green, looking like springtime instead of two weeks shy of Christmas Day.

We arrived at the base of the tower just before nine o'clock, and a queue had already formed. We waited about twenty minutes before reaching the front of the line to buy our tickets to the top of Paris. As we stood under the tower's four wide-spread legs, I had the impression of being inside the belly of some kind of behemoth, and suddenly felt scared, as if I could be crushed.

My fear increased when we crammed into one of the elevators that would pull us up 190 feet to the first floor. As it made its angled climb upward, lifted by pulleys inside one of the tower's metal pillars, I suddenly felt dizzy and lightheaded. My heart started pounding, and I found it difficult to breathe. I looked down through the tower's floorless lattice-like weave of wrought iron, and the ground seemed to peel away like old wallpaper, making me feel raw and exposed. I gripped the handrail, my palms clammy, my knuckles white. My mouth was dry. I couldn't speak, couldn't tell the children to hang on for dear life. But I saw they were safe, delight erupting all over their little faces. The doors opened. I burst out onto the platform, glad to feel something solid beneath my feet.

I had only ever before experienced a fear of falling in a dream. It was a recurring one, usually involving me riding in a large glass box of an elevator, much like the one I had just been in, speeding me high above a city. In my dream the floor always gives way, and I become crazy with fear as I try to press my body against the inside of the rocketing elevator, hoping to somehow stick to the walls. Somehow it always works. I think I will fall, but I never do. It was uncanny—almost the exact imagery, and certainly the same gut-churning terror. Maybe I had been up the Eiffel Tower before and had forgotten? But I knew that wasn't true.

I struggled to compose myself. There was saliva threatening to fall from my bottom lip. I didn't want my children to see, or smell, my fear. I didn't want them to know I felt out of control. I concentrated on the white of the buildings, the blue of the sky. There was a snack bar, and I asked them if they wanted anything. A hot dog, some cake, maybe? They looked at me suspiciously. "We want to go to the top! We want to go to the top!" We boarded a second elevator and rose to 380 feet. I closed my eyes this time because once again I panicked. I thought of the swimming pool, someplace watery and warm and safe. After the third elevator we were at 900 feet, and the wind was so strong I swore I could feel the tower sway. I worried that the children would be blown away, and plummet to their deaths. They thought it extremely funny—me, on my knees, clinging to their coats.

On the observation deck we were caged in, and I derived some comfort from that. But I was afraid to walk along the edges, and didn't want my children to walk along the edges, either. I didn't know what was happening to me, not really, except that it had to do with Paris, and being a mother as well, perhaps. As I had crested high above the rooftops, the city slipping away through me, I had the piercing realization that Paris was my ambition, the goal I had set for myself so many years ago. It seemed to me suddenly to be an unattainable dream. Still, I told myself to hang on, not to give up. That the reach for the top was just as good as getting there. Maybe better.

We went back down to the second platform. The wind was less menacing there. Paris was spread out in every direction, every monument visible and sparkling under a brilliant sun. My son found the *Arc de Triomphe,* proud because he had done so himself. My daughter pointed to the Seine and recalled the boat ride we had taken days before. It was as if they were telling me to relax, enjoy the view. To see the beauty of the city for what it was, unencumbered by thoughts of the past, anxieties about the future. I looked at the city and saw it was made up of straight lines as well as curved ones, journeys that had fixed endings and journeys that meandered indefinitely. I then looked at my two gorgeous, irreplaceable children, smiling at the vista below, and realized that everything I wanted in Paris was right here, right now. In the immediacy of them. I took each by the hand and headed for the elevator, which whooshed us out of the tower and back out onto the street. Immediately we set about looking for a restaurant. Scaling the heights of Paris had made us ravenous. A burning kind of hunger.